Preaching
FROM THE
Prophets

Preaching
FROM THE
Prophets

James Ward
AND
Christine Ward

Abingdon Press
Nashville

PREACHING FROM THE PROPHETS

Copyright © 1995 by Abingdon Press

This book is printed on recycled, acid-free paper.

Library of Congress Cataloging-in-Publication Data

Ward, Christine, 1943–
    Preaching from the prophets/Christine Ward and James M. Ward.
        p.   cm.
    Includes bibliographical references.
    ISBN 0-687-00235-4 (alk. paper)
        1. Bible. O.T. Prophets—Homiletic use.   2. Bible. O.T.
Prophets—Sermons—Outlines, syllabi, etc.   I. Ward, James Merrill,
1928–   . II. Title.
BS1505.5.W37   1995
251—dc20   95-23071
                                                                         CIP

Scripture quotations unless otherwise noted as author translation are from the New Revised Standard Version Bible, Copyright © 1989 by the Division of Christian Education of the National Council of the Churches of Christ in the U.S.A. Used by permission.

95 96 97 98 99 00 01 02 03 04—10 9 8 7 6 5 4 3 2 1

MANUFACTURED IN THE UNITED STATES OF AMERICA

To Karen

CONTENTS

PREFACE

This book is an introductory guide to preaching on texts from the prophetic books of the Bible—Isaiah, Jeremiah, Ezekiel, and the Book of the Twelve Prophets. Although these books have had a decisive impact upon Christian theology during the past century, they have been widely neglected as resources for preaching. The reason for the neglect may be their difficulty, for they are strange and forbidding books. Yet, the prophets were the great preachers of biblical times, and their witness of faith provides a powerful guide and stimulus for the people of God today.

Prophetic preaching, like all human activities, is not timeless, but occurs in a particular time and place and is influenced by its context. That the fingerprints of history mark preaching is unavoidable, but is not to be deplored. Preaching that ministers to the practical needs of the church and the world should be relevant and timely. So should a guidebook on prophetic preaching. Our aim is to offer guidelines for the prophetic preacher today, and we will do so in part by modeling prophetic preaching in our own context. We feel constrained to address certain questions, but we cannot claim to offer final answers, or to have covered all the important questions that preachers in our time should address. Our understanding of prophetic preaching emphasizes the great theological themes of the prophetic writings, which we believe are relevant to all times and situations. However, in expounding these themes in our own social setting, we cannot speak for other men and women in their settings. Everyone must preach his or her own sermons!

The book does not deal systematically with the techniques of preaching or theories of communication. Matters of performance are not the substance of the book. We do commend a particular way of structuring sermons on prophetic texts, because we have found it to be effective in our own experience as preachers. However, that is as far as we go in dealing with the art of preaching itself. But preaching draws not only upon homiletical theory but also upon exegesis and theological interpretation, and it is with these other aspects of preaching that this book is concerned. Our fields of specialization are biblical theology and systematic theology, and we have both done a good deal of preaching from the Bible. Our wish is to share the insights we have gained in interpreting and preaching prophetic texts, and we hope that our book will be useful for seminary courses in preaching as well as for preachers in the church.

The book is dedicated to the Reverend Karen F. Davis, friend and colleague. We are grateful for her encouragement and help on this book.

CHAPTER ONE

Preaching Prophetically and Preaching from the Prophets

P rophetic preaching is crucial to the life and worship of the people of God, because it bears witness to God's grace, which is the foundation of the community's being. Grace redeems us from sin and claims our hearts, minds, and strength for holy living. Prophetic preaching is crucial for the *life* of the community of faith, because it reminds us that a living faith is manifest in works of love and justice. It is crucial for the *worship* of the people of God, because the community is called into being and sustained by the proclamation of the gift and demand of God's grace. The natural inclination of the Christian community, like all religious communities, is to adapt its witness of faith to its most immediate human needs. In doing this the community always runs the risk of obscuring the wider dimensions of the gospel, particularly the wider implications of God's demand for righteousness and justice. What is needed, therefore, is preaching that recovers these wider dimensions and illuminates the ways in which the community obscures them.

Prophetic preaching speaks the word of the living God to the people of God in a particular time and place in the community's historic journey. It is always particular and concrete, the preaching of a particular person as he or she speaks for God and for the covenant community in a specific situation. Each of the biblical prophets faced a distinctive task amid the constant flux of history, and each expressed the gift and demand of God in a distinctive way, which was appropriate to the community's circumstances as well as its covenantal responsibilities.

If it is true that all prophetic preaching is timely and concrete, it is also true that great prophetic preaching is a gift and an art. The biblical prophets display enormous spiritual gifts and high rhetorical art, and so do the famous prophets of other ages. Not everyone can deliver the stirring sermons of an Amos or a Martin Luther King, Jr. Nevertheless, all preachers can learn to incorporate the essential elements of prophetic preaching into his or her own unique proclamation.

When people refer to prophetic preaching, they usually mean preaching that criticizes social injustice and exhorts people to social action. To be sure, prophetic preaching includes these things. However, when it is seen in its fullness, it is much more than these. It is the proclamation of the full gift and demand of God's grace, as it is discerned in the historic pilgrimage of the covenant community. The prophetic preacher witnesses above all to the presence of the living God in the midst of human life. Thus, it is deeply, radically theocentric! The cause that the prophets espouse is the judging and redeeming will of God for the covenant community and for all people.

The true prophet, in the biblical tradition, acts as the conscience of the religious community. The prophet is not an outsider, but an insider who embodies the community's experience and vocation in his or her own life. Thus the prophet is the representative of the community and not merely its critic or adversary. Prophets express the judgment of God, and they experience it in their own life. And, similarly, they not only proclaim God's forgiveness and empowerment, but know it first hand. They are not mechanical instruments of God's communication with the community, but full participants in the community's life, in its aspirations and disappointments as well as its failures and achievements. The prophet is the quintessential Israelite, the paradigmatic covenanter. Deep down, there is no difference between the prophet and the people. In their humanity, their responsibility, and their need, they are one. It is this oneness that makes prophetic preaching possible.

In this book we will be dealing with the contribution that the books of Isaiah, Jeremiah, Ezekiel, and the Twelve Prophets can make to prophetic preaching today. In a sense the whole Bible is prophetic, for the judging and saving word of God comes to the people of God through the whole scriptural witness. However, various parts of the Bible present different problems and possibilities for preaching, and there are advantages to treating them separately. In this case we have chosen to treat the prophets, not only because of their intrinsic merit but because they ordinarily receive less attention in preaching than other parts of the Bible.[1]

The prophetic writings have limitations as resources for preaching that we should acknowledge at the outset. These limitations arise first of all from the great distance between us and the prophets, temporally and culturally. The prophets proclaimed the gift and demand of God's grace in historical settings that were quite unlike our own. We cannot go back to their time and place. The world has changed enormously in the intervening centuries, and so has our knowledge of the world. In addition, the modern preacher is a priest, pastor, and administrator, not simply a prophet. The prophets of ancient Israel did not have to bear these other responsibilities. Therefore, modern preachers cannot merely imitate the Hebrew prophets, but must be prophetic in ways that are appropriate to the full range of their ministerial responsibilities.

Another significant factor affecting our effort to appropriate the message of the prophets is the difference in language. The prophets spoke ancient Hebrew, which is unrelated to the modern Indo-European languages, and their meaning is sometimes obscure to us today. Yet, even as we acknowledge our uncertainty in trying to translate their language into contemporary English, we can take heart in the rhetorical features of the prophetic writings, many of which can be carried over into contemporary preaching. Their vivid metaphors and poetic cadences, for example, invite emulation. There is much in these books to draw upon in crafting sermons today, in both their literary expression and their theological content.

We are convinced that the witness of the prophets remains immensely relevant to the life and faith of the covenant community today. The preaching of the prophets deals much of the time with fundamental issues of religious faith and human relations, and not only with particular aspects of the life of ancient Israel. The task of the modern preacher is to discern within the prophetic writings the fundamental understanding of the gift and demand of God's grace that informs them, and to proclaim this understanding anew in our time, with conviction and imagination.

Among the resources for our understanding and witness contained in the prophetic books, the reports of the prophets' experiences of God's call stand out. Here the gift and demand of God's grace are experienced concretely and personally, and the life of faithful obedience is exemplified. It is not only the actual call-reports that are relevant here (Isa. 6; Jer. 1; Ezek. 1–3; Hos. 1; and Amos 7:10-17), but also the direct and indirect indications of the personal experience of the prophets as they fulfilled their vocation, reflected upon it, and drew out its implications for the understanding of Israel's relationship with God. Chief among the qualities of their experience is its profound sense of the presence of God. The prophets lived a life of radical God-centeredness consistent with the God-centeredness of their message, and their life of faithful devotion lends authenticity to their message.

Despite their extraordinary personal experience of God's presence, the prophets were not isolated individuals but participated fully in the religious and social life of Israel. Indeed, the immediacy of their encounter with God prompted them to engage intensely with others in the community. In doing this the prophets addressed the crucial social and religious questions of their time. They did so with courage and candor.

While some of our modern questions do not receive direct answers from the prophetic writings, we can learn to appropriate the wisdom of the prophets, as well as to model their faithfulness to God and God's call upon their lives. The rapid social change that we experience today, and that continues to take us further and further away from the world of the prophets, is not unlike the social upheaval the prophets experienced themselves. As their world altered, swiftly and catastrophically, they were impelled to proclaim the ancient covenantal faith in new ways, and in the process they discovered new dimensions of that faith, which had not been perceived as clearly before. So it is with the modern interpreter of the faith. Preaching today requires insight and imagination to proclaim the ancient faith authentically, but also in new ways which take into account the new problems and possibilities in the human experience and in the covenant community.

This book is designed with a single purpose in mind: to show the kind of contribution the prophetic books can make to Christian preaching today. It will do this as concretely and practically as possible, by considering specific topics of preaching in relation to particular biblical texts. This will be done in chapters 4 and 5, which make up the bulk of the book. Chapters 2 and 3 deal with several general questions that are fundamental to the task of preaching from prophetic texts. In chapter 2 the relation of the witness of faith of the prophets to the Christian witness of faith is discussed. This is a question that is implicit in any Christian preaching on texts from the Hebrew Bible and ought to be explicit in the mind of the preacher. Chapter 3 deals with the practical questions of how to choose texts from among the vast array of possibilities in the prophetic books, and how to develop sermons once the texts have been chosen.

The two final chapters suggest two different approaches to preaching on prophetic texts. In chapter 4 we begin with the biblical text and work forward to the contemporary situation, while in chapter 5 we start with the contemporary situation and work back to the biblical text. The difference is somewhat artificial because both movements, from situation to text and from text to situation, are involved in any preaching that is both faithful to the biblical witness and relevant to our life today. Nevertheless, it is possible to emphasize one or the other of these two movements.

The themes treated in chapter 4 deal primarily with God's love of us and our love of God, and those in chapter 5 deal primarily with our love of neighbor and all God's creatures. Once again there is a certain artificiality in the distinction, because according to the witness of the prophets, as well as the Christian witness, a vital faith is always manifest in works of love and righteousness that spring from our love of God. Nevertheless, it is possible to emphasize one or the other of these two aspects of our witness, the "theological" or the "ethical."

In each chapter we do three things: first, we discuss the methodological problems involved in the task at hand; next we survey a number of texts relevant to the themes being considered; and finally, we offer concise sermons on specific texts. These are not complete sermons because they do not include the introductions and concrete illustrations that would make them fully relevant to the life of a particular congregation and give them the immediacy of oral communication. In a sense they are penultimate drafts. Many have been preached in United Methodist churches in Oklahoma, Texas, and Louisiana. In content these are the kinds of sermons that are authentic for us and that we have preached for many years. But they are not the final sermon! Neither of us preaches from a manuscript, for we believe preaching to be a creative, oral event involving the preacher, the congregation, and the Holy Spirit. Moreover, while the sermons offered here express the substance of what we would preach on these texts, we preach quite differently from each other in the actual event of preaching. Our intention in presenting these sermons is to stimulate and encourage preaching from the prophets by others. Preachers must engage the biblical text and the contemporary situation in a way that is authentic for them in creating their own sermons. Each of our sermons illustrates just one possible way of appropriating the message of a particular prophetic text.

CHAPTER TWO

Prophetic Preaching and Theological Perspective

Every preacher, like every other interpreter of scripture, is responsible for the theological perspective that informs his or her practical work of ministry. By theological perspective we mean the fundamental theological viewpoint from which one interprets the whole of life and which shapes one's understanding of scripture and the situation in which one preaches. Everyone has a theological perspective, whether or not he or she is fully aware of it. The clearer we are about our basic perspective, the better able we will be to reclaim the biblical witness in a valid way for the church today. Our preaching must not merely repeat the witness of the past, but must appropriate the biblical witness in terms that affirm God's sovereign grace and empower the faithful witness and service of Christian people living at our time in human history.

At the heart of our theological perspective is an understanding of the three-fold reality at the center of Christian life, the complex reality of God, Jesus Christ, and the church, the covenant community that is sent into the world in Jesus' name. But before sketching our understanding of this reality, we need to say something about theological language, particularly the language of the biblical writers, and about the impact of history upon our theological perspective.

Theological Language

The prophetic oracles contain many metaphors for God that challenge our theological understanding and our preaching. For example, what do we make of Jeremiah's characterization of God as a "deceitful brook"? The prophets borrowed images from a wide range of human experiences and the world of nature to talk about people's relation to God. They were quintessential makers of metaphors. Clearly, they felt free to speak of God and God's relation to human beings in vivid and concrete ways. Yet we must understand their metaphors for what they are and not turn them into literal assertions about the nature of God. The theological metaphors of the prophets—and other biblical writers—point to realities in the covenant community's experience of God—they are objective in this sense—but at the same time they speak of realities that cannot be fully grasped in human language, that is, of God and human existence before God. When Jeremiah calls God "a deceitful brook," we assume that he is speaking about his experience of reality, that is, of something real in his relationship with God. But in this case we understand readily that he does not mean literally that God is a stream of water. There are many other metaphors of God like this one in the books of the prophets, such as lion, rock, and moth. However, human metaphors for God, such as judge, king, lord, husband, friend, mother, and father, are much more challenging for the preacher. Some of these metaphors are so firmly fixed in our religious language and so deeply embedded in our consciousness that many people no longer think of them as metaphors but as literal descriptions of God.[1]

The reason this aspect of prophetic language is so challenging today is that most of the metaphors are male. Female metaphors are used, but only rarely. The vast majority of metaphors for God in the prophetic books, as well as throughout the Bible, are male. This usage, of course, reflects the patriarchal structure of Israelite society. Within that framework, the people in authority in every sector of life were men; thus God was depicted characteristically as warrior, king, father, lord, and the like. However, we realize today that the continual use of male metaphors for God, from biblical times until our own, has suggested that there is a closer connection between God and men than there is between God and women. As a result, discrimination against women and exclusion of women from aspects of the church's life and ministry have been justified in the minds of many.

Thus, while metaphors drawn from our human relationships are helpful, even indispensable, in speaking about God, we should avoid absolutizing any of this language. Our theological language is always our creation, and we bear responsibility for it. The modern preacher has a moral obligation not to speak of God in ways that contribute to the suffering of others but to speak in ways that enable the word of God to become a living reality for every man and woman. We believe that any preaching from the prophets today that is oblivious to the influence of patriarchy upon the biblical texts contradicts in principle the prophets' demand for justice in the human community, even though the prophets themselves were not aware of their cultural conditioning in this regard. Understood properly, and used with care, the metaphorical language of the prophets need not be a stumbling block for us, but an invitation to preach as creatively in our time as the prophets did in theirs. It is crucial, therefore, that we continually mix our theological metaphors.

Theological Perspective and Historical Context

Our theological perspective is shaped by our life experience. We recognize that all human activities, including bearing witness to the living God through prophetic preaching, reflect the time and place in history in which they occur. Thus we understand God and what God requires of us, as persons shaped by the events of the twentieth century. One of these events is the movement among socially disadvantaged groups to understand their situation and to overcome the forces of injustice that control their lives. For example, our participation in the U. S. civil rights movement affected our theological perspective and our Christian witness. As a result we became aware that social structures can be oppressive and unjust for disadvantaged people.

Thus we welcome the rich diversity of theological viewpoints that informs scriptural interpretation and preaching today. This richness enables voices to be heard that were previously silent or excluded from mainstream biblical interpretation—the voices of women, people of color, the poor, and others who are socially disadvantaged. We rejoice in this diversity and wish to take advantage of it as much as possible in this book. But each group speaks distinctively, in its own accents, out of its own experience, and with its own emphases. Since we cannot presume to speak for others, our responsibility here is to acknowledge the theological perspective that informs our own preaching.

Another factor emerging from events of the twentieth century that affects our witness is the recognition of the Christian complicity in the Holocaust. Our recognition has been stimulated particularly by the writings of survivors of the Holocaust like Elie Wiesel and Emil Fackenheim.[2] The causes of this complicity are many and will perhaps never be fully understood. Yet, we are convinced that one important cause has been the church's supersessionist interpretation of the prophetic writings. According to this interpretation, Christianity superseded—displaced—Judaism as the true covenant community, in fulfillment of prophecy. This interpretation, which presupposes that Judaism is a failed religion, is no longer acceptable today. The Jewish community has existed as a vital religious community through the centuries. As Christians and fellow heirs of God's covenant with ancient Israel, we affirm that Judaism has been preserved by God's grace in the face of horrendous treatment by gentiles. We cannot preach faithfully from prophetic texts and at the same time ignore the reality of Jewish history or the reality of Christian anti-Semitism. In this regard Protestants can learn from Roman Catholic efforts since the Second Vatican Council about reshaping Christian attitudes toward Judaism.[3]

The Holocaust and the recent civil rights movement among disadvantaged people are just two of the events of the twentieth century that have defined the context of our witness and made it impossible for us merely to repeat the witness of Christians as it was expressed in previous centuries. All preaching, including our own, is affected by history, both personal and communal, and the preacher should take full account of this fact.

Our theological perspective, then, is shaped by our life experience in this century, but it is not simply relative to our experience. The theological perspective we bring to bear on the task of prophetic preaching is grounded in the church's witness of faith in Jesus Christ. We speak first of all as persons who know the grace of God through Jesus Christ, and we speak above all to other Christian preachers. At the same time, we intend our interpretation of the biblical texts to be faithful to the prophets' own witness, and we do not intend in any way to undermine the Jewish witness of faith.

We turn now to the three-fold reality at the heart of the Christian life and witness: God, Jesus Christ, and the church.

Who Is God?

The understanding of God that we share is that God is not detached from the world in which we live but is intimately and continuously involved in the whole of creation. The living God did not simply create the world and then abandon it sometime in the distant past! God continuously creates and sustains creaturely life and seeks to redeem and hallow the lives of all people everywhere. No man or woman is either the self-sufficient creator of his or her own destiny or the mere victim of fate. God's judging and redeeming grace is nearer to all men and women than life itself, and God's voice speaks to each of us through the voice of our conscience, calling us to love God and our neighbors as ourselves, even though we reject God's love again and again and fail to live lives that honor God.

God has not acted in the lives of all peoples in just the same way, even though God loves all people. Rather, God has acted in history in distinctive ways to create and re-create the covenant community—ancient Israel and its descendants, Christianity, Judaism, and Islam. God's self-disclosure in history, beginning with the history of ancient Israel, is the foundation of the community's witness of faith. The members of this community do not differ from other men and women in their humanity. They are no more beloved by God and certainly no less sinful than other people. But God's self-disclosure in history re-creates them as a new people with a special vocation. Their vocation is defined by responsibility to obey God's torah—teaching, law— and to be a light to the nations, that is, to bear witness to God's righteous and gracious love amid the many peoples and cultures of the world. Christianity, Judaism, and Islam do this in different ways. Christians alone bear witness to God's gracious act in Jesus Christ.

Who Is Jesus?

Christians know God as "the God and father of our lord Jesus Christ." Jesus is the one through whom God saves us and creates the covenant community called the church. Jesus is not merely a prophet, although he proclaimed the same gift and demand of God's grace as the prophets. Nor is he a mere role model. He is irreplaceable in the church's witness as the sacrament of God's grace, the one through whose life, death, and resurrection God created the church. Jesus is, in Martin Luther's words, "the man of God's own choosing." He is the one through whom Christians uniquely come to know God and the one to whom they bear witness.

Throughout the church's history Christians have proclaimed their faith in Jesus Christ using a variety of christologies of witness. By christologies of witness we do not mean the church's doctrinal formulations but the spontaneous christologies used by Christians to testify to their experience of God's grace. The New Testament writers speak of Jesus as Lamb, Word of God, Lord, Savior, Son of man, Son of God, bread of life, Son of David, and, of course, Messiah (christos). These titles all refer to the depth and breadth of the relationship between Jesus and those bearing witness to him. Again, they are various ways of expressing the Christian experience of God's redemption through Jesus Christ. We believe that a particularly fitting christology of witness for our time is Paul's christology of reconciliation, as it is expressed for example in 2 Cor. 5:19-20: "In Christ God was reconciling the world to himself, not counting their trespasses against them, and entrusting the message of reconciliation to us. So we are ambassadors for Christ, since God is making his appeal through us; we entreat you on behalf of Christ, be reconciled to God."

The Church

When we speak of the church we do not mean any particular institutional structure. Rather we mean the fellowship of men and women who have known the gift and demand of God's grace through Jesus Christ, throughout the world and down through the centuries, and who are called to bear witness to their faith to all the world. As we have said, the church is a distinctive descendant of the covenant community of ancient Israel. In calling men and women to the church, God saves us from sin and sets us free to witness to Jesus Christ by loving God and all those whom God loves from the depths of our experience. The church alone is appointed to preach the gospel of God's love, to embody God's love communally, and to strive for healing and reconciliation in the broken world around us *in Jesus' name*. In other words, the church, **the body of Christ,** is the sacrament of God's love as it is known through Jesus Christ.

The Church and the Jewish Community

Jesus and his first disciples, those who were present with him during his Galilean ministry, his passion, death, and resurrection, were all Jews. Jesus himself remained a faithful Jew throughout his life, and his disciples responded to his teaching, his life, and his death as Jews. It was the church and the synagogue that severed relations with each other and bequeathed to later generations the legacy of separateness and mutual distrust. Moreover, we are convinced that the similarities between the witness of the Hebrew prophets and that of the apostles are deeper and more extensive than many preachers of the Bible are prone to admit. Both prophets and apostles spoke of God's judging and redeeming presence, and called men and women to repent and turn to God and one another in love and trust. To be sure, there is a crucial difference between the two that cannot be overlooked. The Hebrew prophets knew the gift and claim of God's grace through ancient Israel's life as God's people, particularly through its birth as a community in the deliverance of the exodus and the covenant-making at Sinai. The apostles knew the same gift and demand of God's grace but in a new way. Through the event of Jesus Christ—the life, death, and resurrection of Jesus, the Jew of Nazareth—God created a new, reconciled and reconciling community, the church, alongside the community of Judaism.

The church knows God first of all through the event of Jesus Christ. Judaism knows God through the covenantal events of Israel's history, from the call of Abraham to the exodus from Egypt and the sealing of the covenant at Sinai, to the renewal of covenantal life in the rabbinical period, down to the rebirth of the state of Israel in the twentieth century. Christians also know God through the ancient covenantal events, but they are the adopted children of Israel, or, to use Paul's metaphor, branches grafted into the trunk of Israel (Rom. 9–11). Again, the church, like modern Judaism, is a direct descendant of the covenant community of ancient Israel.

In the aftermath of the terrible suffering of the Jewish community in the twentieth century, which was largely at the hands of people educated by the church, we believe it is crucial for Christians to remember that Christians have not replaced Jews as the people of God. Christians have been added to the one covenant community, grafted onto the tree of Abraham. The several branches of the religious community of Israel today, like the many denominations that make up the church universal, are distinctive forms of God's covenant people. We do not minimize the many differences between Judaism and Christianity with regard to scripture, ritual practice, and communal life.[4] We affirm that both were created by God's judging and redeeming love, and that God's love places the same comprehensive claim over the lives of Jews and Christians alike. We are all called to love God with our whole being and to love all those whom God loves. God promises never to abandon the covenant people, and God's righteous and gracious presence continues to redeem and bless us all throughout our different historic journeys.

Preaching from the Prophets

A prophetic sermon preached in the Christian community calls men and women to the God of Jesus Christ and thus more deeply into the community of the church, whether the sermon is preached on a text from the New Testament or one from the Hebrew Bible. The God who speaks through a prophetic sermon preached in the church is known to Christians through the event of Jesus Christ, and also through the redemptive events in the life of ancient Israel. The same God is made known in the experience of ancient Israel as in the experience of the church, and the same gift and demand of God's grace are proclaimed in the prophetic writings as in the New Testament. The fundamental understanding of God's love and mercy, God's righteousness and judgment that informs the Hebrew prophets, psalmists, and writers of the Torah, is the same as that which informs the writers of the New Testament. That is the reason why the New Testament writings are so filled with Old Testament quotations and allusions and are so permeated by its ideas. As a consequence of this profound theological unity of the scriptures, the Christian preacher does not have to mention Jesus or the New Testament explicitly in a sermon on a prophetic text in order for the sermon to bear witness to the truth about God and ourselves before God.[5]

CHAPTER THREE

Choosing
Texts and
Developing Sermons

Choosing Prophetic Texts

Together, the prophetic books are as long and diverse as the entire New Testament, and they were composed over a far longer period of time and in a much greater variety of settings. As a result of this sheer length and complexity, the task of choosing texts that are truly representative of the witness of the prophets and, at the same time, suitable for preaching today, can be daunting.

For those who follow the Revised Common Lectionary the range of prophetic texts is drastically reduced. Nevertheless, one still needs a rationale to guide one's choice. The selection of prophetic texts in the Revised Common Lectionary has both strengths and weaknesses. On one hand, the individual texts express important aspects of the prophetic witness and are appropriate texts for preaching. On the other hand, the number of texts is relatively small, compared to the number in the prophetic books themselves, and the selection is shaped by the church's liturgical calendar. Texts from the Old Testament are paired with New Testament texts in such a way that the Hebrew Bible is represented as a promise, for which Jesus Christ is the fulfillment, and his birth, passion, crucifixion, and resurrection are the controlling motifs of the selection. Quite apart from the question of whether this practice misrepresents the message of the Old Testament texts, the message of the prophetic writings is far richer than the Revised Common Lectionary suggests.

Therefore, we recommend that it be used critically, as an aid in choosing texts for preaching, but not as the sole determinant.[1]

Some of the texts singled out for sermons in this book are included in the Revised Common Lectionary and some are not. All of them were chosen because they are representative of the prophetic witness and are relevant to Christian witness today. The reasons for particular choices will be given later, but the two stated above are the main principles governing our selection. Thus, texts should be chosen that truly represent the witness—or message—of the prophetic writings themselves. This means they should express theological or ethical ideas that are integral to the thought of the books in which they are found, and are not merely tangential ideas. It also means that the preacher should exercise care when dealing with ideas that are expressed only once or twice in the prophetic corpus and are thus not really representative of the broader prophetic tradition. The second guiding principle is that texts should be chosen whose message can be genuinely affirmed, or validly interpreted and appropriated, within the context of the life and witness of the people of God today. This does not mean that ideas should be filtered out which do not conform to our own, or that are likely to be unpopular with our hearers, but that we must take responsibility for interpreting the biblical message in our own time. We will have more to say about the task of interpretation in the next two chapters.

A major consideration in selecting prophetic texts for use in preaching is to take into account the relation of the ideas expressed in a particular text with those expressed in its canonical context. How does the message contained in the text relate to that of the book in which it stands? How does the surrounding material affect the meaning of the chosen text? If this relation of text and context is ignored, the text may become a mere pretext for a sermon, having little real relation to it.

When we speak about the message of the prophets, first of all we mean the message, or messages, of the individual prophets. Each one expressed his understanding of God's gift and demand in a particular way and in a particular time and place. No two prophets said exactly the same thing. Therefore, the message of each prophet should be viewed in its individual configuration and in relation to its own historic setting, if the message is to be understood as fully as possible. Amos and Hosea prophesied in pre-exilic Israel during the eighth century B.C.E.; Micah and First Isaiah in Judah during the same era; Zephaniah, Nahum, Habakkuk, and Jeremiah during the late pre-exilic and exilic eras in Judah; Ezekiel and the writer of Isaiah 40–55 in exile in Babylonia during the sixth century; Joel, Haggai, Zechariah, Malachi, and the writers of Isaiah 56–66 in post-exilic Judea during the fifth and fourth centuries.

The first thing to do, then, in order to make an informed choice about which prophetic texts to use for preaching, is to discern their meaning and purpose, as much as possible, in their original settings. But this is not the only thing to do. The texts all come to us in redacted form, the end product of a process of selection, combination, and expansion within the Judean community between the seventh and fourth centuries B.C.E. Therefore, in order to understand particular prophetic texts more fully, we read them in relation to the larger, redacted works of which they are a part, and, beyond that, in relation to the whole corpus of writings that make up the prophetic division of the canon. When all this is done, we will not only understand the message of a particular text better, but we will also be in a better position to decide how representative it is of the prophetic canon as a whole.[2] This process is illustrated in the preliminary comments accompanying the sermons in chapters 4 and 5. Placing a text in its canonical context in this way requires basic knowledge of the contents and growth of the prophetic books but not the advanced knowledge of a biblical specialist.

The Form of the Text and the Form of the Sermon

We speak about the *message* of the texts because it is the primary factor in selecting texts for preaching. Yet, every text comes to us in a particular *literary form* with a particular structure, and we must decide, when preaching on a text, whether to follow its structure in constructing our sermon. This is an issue because most of the prophetic texts were not constructed for the same purposes as modern sermons; therefore, their structures may not serve our purposes well.[3]

In speaking of the literary form of the text we are not referring here to the words, phrases, or figures of speech contained in a text but to its overall structure, its sequence of ideas. The words, phrases, and figures of speech of the prophets are usually vivid and memorable, and it may be rhetorically effective to use the actual language of the text in one's sermon. But adopting the structure of the prophetic text may not be equally effective, since the structures were created for communication in settings quite different from ours and, very likely, for different purposes. It is the contemporary setting and purpose of the sermon that should determine its structure and not the structure of the ancient text. If the structure of the text happens to be appropriate to the modern setting, and to the homiletical intentions of the preacher, then it might well be followed in the construction of the sermon. But if it is not, then there is no good reason to imitate it. Recognizing and analyzing the form or structure of the prophet's communication is always a good thing to do, for it enhances understanding of the message; but once this has been done, the preacher is free to use the prophet's message as a resource without being limited by the structure of the text.

Prophetic texts exhibit a great variety of literary types. The most common type, particularly among the pre-exilic, poetic oracles (i.e., those of Amos, Hosea, Isaiah, Micah, Zephaniah, Habakkuk, and Jeremiah), is the two-part prophecy of God's punishment of Israel because of its unrighteousness. One part is the *accusation* of unrighteousness—usually idolatry, apostasy, or injustice—and the other is the *threat* of God's judgment—typically as a prophecy of the decline or destruction of the nation or its leaders. The number of creative variations on this simple form in the prophetic books is remarkable. The question then arises as to whether this form, which is so prominent in the prophetic corpus, is not a legitimate one to adopt in shaping a contemporary sermon. On the whole it is *not* an appropriate form to adopt, if what is communicated is simply a denuncia-tion of evil and threat of God's judgment. If these themes of the prophetic proclamation are included in the sermon, they should be balanced by an affirmation of God's grace. The knowledge of God's redeeming love—which is the fundamental message of the covenantal tradition, and which is reaffirmed in the gospel of

Jesus Christ—must be clearly recognized as the ultimate basis of judgment. Such a procedure would be true to both the prophetic witness and the Christian witness.

[Oracles of judgment and oracles of salvation]are the two most common types of writing, or genres, in the prophetic literature, but there are many others, including several that are not prophetic genres at all, but were borrowed for prophetic use from other settings: songs, prayers, proverbial sayings, laments, curses, hymns, and so on. These other genres do not readily lend themselves to the formal requirements of a sermon, though any text can be cited in a sermon if it contains an appropriate idea and is not merely a pretext.

The oracles of judgment, with their motifs of accusation and threat, dominate the collections of pre-exilic prophetic writings. These oracles are poetry and they are mostly quite brief (though they are combined into rather lengthy series of oracles in the canonical books as we have them). This short, poetic form is ideally suited to the kinds of occasions referred to in Isaiah 7, Amos 7, and Jeremiah 7 and 26, which provide the most explicit information we have about the situations in which the pre-exilic prophets prophesied. Short, arresting oracles in poetry were appropriate, and perhaps necessary, in such settings, for the prophets appear to have been uninvited and unwelcome, and presumably did not have time to speak at greater length. What was required was an utterance that got the hearer's attention quickly and was easily remembered. Their oracles were like the modern sermon in that they were delivered orally rather than in writing, but they differed from the typical modern sermon in most other respects. They were only a fraction of the length, and they were composed in poetry. A concise, poetic oracle is not the type of communication appropriate ordinarily for a sermon in church or synagogue, though it might be used as part of a longer, prose sermon.

When the prophets were denied an audience, or when Israel ceased to exist as a nation, they used other kinds of communication appropriate to the new circumstances. After he was barred from prophesying in the temple of Jerusalem, Jeremiah engaged a scribe to write down his oracles on a scroll, which was then delivered for reading in the hearing of the Judean king

(Jer. 36). After the fall of the nation and the dispersion of its survivors in Egypt, Babylon, and elsewhere, new kinds of prophetic communication were created. Second Isaiah wrote lengthy poems of consolation and exhortation, probably for reading among the exiles. Anonymous disciples of Jeremiah composed sermonic speeches in prose, which resemble the modern sermon stylistically (e.g., Jer. 7:1–8:13 and 11:1-14). This kind of communication has persisted in use in synagogues and churches essentially unchanged for over two thousand years. Obviously, then, these prose sermonic texts are the most natural models for adaptation in contemporary preaching. The other prophetic genres presuppose a quite different social setting, and, therefore, a quite different relationship between audience and speaker, and they are not as useful, formally, for the crafting of sermons today.

There are many effective ways to structure sermons, and everyone discovers by trial and error which forms are most effective for themselves. The conventional form has long been the *topical sermon*, consisting typically of three points with an introduction and conclusion. This is a useful model, but it requires skillful development of the individual points if it is not to be monotonous. The structure itself, as distinguished from the content, is static, in constrast to the dynamic character of the two following forms.

In our judgment, the *narrative sermon* is usually more effective than an ordinary topical sermon. A narrative has dramatic movement—a beginning, a middle, and an end—which naturally engages the imagination of the congregation. It awakens expectations and holds interest more easily than a purely topical format. By narrative sermon we do not mean one that includes illustrations or anecdotes in story form, but one that is constructed as a narrative.[4]

The way a narrative sermon works is self-evident. It begins by describing a scene, an event, or a human situation, and it goes on to tell what happens, until the outcome of the story is reached, and the listeners' expectations are satisfied. Narrative preaching is widely commended because it allows the preacher to manage the tension and drama of prophetic oracles, and is suited to many other biblical texts as well.

Another form that we find particularly suitable for construct-ing sermons from prophetic texts has three parts: *the problem, the resolution,* and *the new possibility.* Like the narrative sermon, it has a beginning, middle, and end; however, these are of a particular sort. First, the problem is described, and it is ordinar-ily a significant moral, social, or spiritual problem that the people in the congregation encounter in their lives. Secondly, a means of resolving the problem is proposed; that is to say, an answer to the human dilemma is suggested, which grows out of the biblical witness of faith and is usually related to grace, opening up new possibilities for the hallowing of life. Finally, some of these possibilities for the life of faith are affirmed. This structure is particularly suited to sermons on prophetic texts, because many of these texts have the same structure.

Isaiah 6 can be employed to illustrate these three sermon structures: the topical, the narrative, and the problem-resolu-tion-new possibility structure. A three-point *topical sermon* on Isaiah's famous call to prophecy might speak about God as sovereign, as holy, and as redeeming, with an appropriate intro-duction and conclusion. This structure would be a valid exposi-tion of the ideas contained in the text. However, it would eliminate the dramatic development of the prophet's own pres-entation. The individual points might be well made, but the overall structure would not have the force of the original, because it would not heighten the awesome experience of God's call. Consequently, the structure of the sermon would be essen-tially repetitious, however different the contents of the individ-ual points might be. The rhetorical effectiveness of the sermon would depend entirely on the way in which each individual point was made. The structure of the sermon would contribute little to its impact.

By contrast, the other two kinds of structure we have de-scribed contribute to the impact of the sermon because they have an organic—dramatic, internally logical—development that the purely topical form lacks. Each part requires the next part to complete its intention, until the last part brings the whole to a close. An expectation created at the beginning, either by the narrative description of a human situation or by the posing of a human problem, is satisfied by the completion of the story or the resolution of the problem. The listener's attention is grasped early in the sermon and is held throughout, until the plot—narrative or problematic—is fully completed. If the plot is interesting or the problem real, the structure of the sermon cannot fail to contribute to the listener's engagement. The effect of the plot would be lessened, of course, if the treatment of it were boring or inept. However, if the parts were treated effectively at all, the overall structure of the plot would enhance their effect.

A *narrative sermon* on Isaiah 6 might tell the story of God and the kingdom of Judah as Isaiah interpreted it, or the story of God and Isaiah, the prophet. Both are highly dramatic stories with significant religious outcomes, and both are exemplified in this text. The historic destiny of the unholy kingdom of Judah, under the sovereignty of the holy God, is proclaimed here. It leads through national disaster to the possibility of new life. Simultaneously, Isaiah's destiny as a prophet of God is characterized, from the conviction of his sinfulness before the holy God, and his forgiveness and commissioning as a prophet, to his recognition of the terrible outcome of his preaching, that is, the hardening of the people's hearts. Both stories, that of the kingdom and that of the prophet, could be told in such a way that their relevance to the life of faith today would be evident, without compromising their integrity as biblical stories.

A *problem-resolution-new possibility* sermon on this text might have a similar conclusion to that of the narrative sermon, but it would reach it by a shorter, more obvious route. Instead of telling the whole story, from beginning to end, it would focus on the main human problem represented in the text (Israel's unrighteousness before the holy God), its resolution (the disastrous dissolution of the kingdom), and the resulting human possibilities (the holy seed).

How many *points* are made in a narrative or problem-resolution-new possibility sermon? The number of points in a topical sermon is usually clear because the structure itself is a series of points. But the number is not so clear in the other two types of sermons. If the sermon is a narrative it will contain as many *points* as it takes to complete the narrative. To take another concrete example from the prophets, if one were preaching on Jeremiah 26, which narrates at some length the incident of

Jeremiah's prophesying in the temple of Jerusalem in 604 B.C.E., one might emphasize five or six moments in the account, and draw out the appropriate inferences. This particular narrative requires little explicit application by the preacher because the situation it describes, that is, the negative reaction of clergy to criticism by laity, is so common in the religious community that the listeners can make the application themselves.

When the plot of the sermon is based on a human problem and its resolution, the development of the plot is at least two-fold—problem and resolution—but it may better be three-fold: the human problem, the means of resolution, and the new possibilities or outcome. This three-fold structure resembles the structure of a story—beginning, middle, and end—and, therefore, has greater dramatic power than a two-fold one. The problem posed can be any moral, spiritual, or social problem that we experience, and that is suggested by the biblical text on which we are preaching. The means of resolution of the problem would ordinarily be some aspect of God's grace or redemptive action. The new possibility would include the responsibility laid upon us by grace, as well as the gift bestowed by it. We have adopted this problem-resolution-new possibility structure much of the time in the illustrative sermons in chapters 4 and 5. The primary reason for doing so is that it conforms to the essential structure of the prophetic texts that have been selected.

CHAPTER FOUR

Preaching
on the Themes
of the Prophets

The preacher stands between the biblical text and the contemporary situation as interpreter of God's word for the community of faith today. The dialogue between text and situation is genuinely two-way. The Bible not only addresses our situation, but is addressed by it. In this chapter and the next we deal with the homiletical task of engaging text and situation in dialogue with one another. In this chapter we take the text as the starting point and move from text to contemporary situation, while in the following chapter we reverse the procedure, beginning with issues relevant to our contemporary situation and moving back to the biblical text. This chapter is divided into three parts. The first considers the general question of beginning with the text, the second sketches the main themes of the prophetic books, and the third deals with the development of sermons on representative prophetic texts.

Beginning with the Text

The first question we might ask ourselves is why begin a contemporary sermon with an ancient prophetic text. The answer lies in the nature of the prophetic corpus. This body of literature was compiled because the prophets' preaching had sustained the people of God through historical change and upheaval for over four hundred years, and because it was so profoundly centered on God. God and God's relationship with human beings are the explicit subjects of the entire prophetic corpus. Furthermore, the prophets' own intimate relationship with God enabled them to speak for God to the covenant community—as well as for the community to God—and to discern what God intended and required for their lives. We live in a different age, but the covenant community in our age has a deep need to know what God intends for us and what God requires of us. The proclamation of the ancient prophets can illuminate our need and direct our path. If preachers wishing to be prophetic today never begin their reflections with texts from the prophets, they run the risk of a narrow focus on immediate needs and a loss of theological perspective. The prophets can save us from self-interest and superficiality. They focus our attention on the things that matter most.

At the same time, there are dangers in beginning *always* with the ancient text. The preacher's responsibility is to stand as interpreter between the biblical text and the contemporary situation, and if the preacher always begins with the text and never with the situation, pressing contemporary problems that were not addressed by the ancient prophets may go unaddressed. One of the hallmarks of the prophets was that they reappropriated the prophetic tradition afresh in each new time and place, and took the risk of proclaiming a new word of God. One is struck by the historical concreteness of so many of the prophetic oracles, though on reflection it becomes clear that they are grounded in the enduring reality of God's purpose. A similar combination of timeliness and depth is what is needed from the present-day preacher.

Many passages in the books of the prophets are suitable for preaching. In fact, few are totally lacking in homiletical possibilites. However, it is better to choose texts on the basis of a clear rationale than to choose them arbitrarily. First of all, the sermon will be more effective rhetorically. And secondly, a more appropriate understanding of the prophetic books will be communicated to the congregation. The prophetic books are not card-files of sermon texts with no relation to one another but works of literature with their own integrity. As already stated, the preacher needs appropriate principles of selection. The principle employed in this chapter is to choose texts that are representative of the major themes of the prophetic proclamation. Therefore, let us now give a brief résumé of those themes.

The Themes of the Prophetic Witness

The prophetic writings are consistently theological, in the sense that they are always about God. The prophets' oracles are presented as the word of God, and their reflections on their relationship with God are expressed in direct address to God. Thus, nearly everything a prophet says is in the form of divine-human dialogue. However, the prophets' writings do not provide a full exposition of their understanding of God. Some aspects of their understanding are merely implicit in what they wrote, though these can be inferred from a comprehensive study of their writings.

In the prophetic understanding, God is known first of all in covenantal relationship. The prophets addressed God and spoke for God as Yahweh, the God of Israel, whose name, indicative of God's nature (i.e., in the revelation to Moses: "I will be who I will be," [Exod. 3:14]), became known in the formative events of covenantal history (Exod. 3:13-17; 6:2-9). There are many allusions to the covenantal traditions in the prophetic books, though most of the time these traditions are simply presupposed by the prophets. (We should remember, of course, that the Torah in the form we know it in the Bible was compiled later than most of the prophetic books). God's self-disclosure in calling and forming Israel into a covenant community is the foundation of the prophets' knowledge of God, and the foundation of their proclamation of God's renewal of the covenant community after the destruction of the Israelite kingdoms. This is the first theme to be treated in this chapter, in the section entitled *God's Presence Made Known in Israel's History.*

God's covenant with Israel is a gift, but it involves responsibility. A great many prophetic oracles accuse Israel of failing to fulfill its responsibility to God and to the other members of the covenant community and proclaim the negative consequences of that failure, namely, the judgment of God. Other oracles promise God's renewal of the covenant relationship, after the experience of judgment. These themes dominate the prophetic books. In the process of proclaiming them, the prophets also disclose the theological foundations of their witness.

The prophetic witness of faith is radically monotheistic. Although it is only in Isaiah 40–55 that one finds a full articulation of this monotheism, it is implied in all the prophetic books. All the prophetic oracles are passionate appeals to the reality and sovereignty of the one true God, and no prophet makes any concession to an alternative view.

The implications of this radical monotheism are important. First of all, God is regarded as ultimately sovereign over the world and all its inhabitants. The prophets do not speak about the world of nature nearly as often as they do about the human world, but when they do it is clear that they consider nature subject to God's power just as human beings are. Other nations, and not just Israel, are subject to God's righteous rule, even though they do not share Israel's special knowledge and service of God. Most of the oracles concerning foreign nations criticize them for pretentious pride and the abuse of other peoples (Isa. 13–23; Jer. 46–51; Ezek. 25–32; Amos 1–2), but there are a few oracles that give them a positive place in God's saving work (e.g., Isa. 19:19-25; 45:1-7; Amos 9:7). The second theme to be treated in this chapter, *The Boundaries of God's Love*, concerns God's relation to non-Israelite people.

Another implication of the prophets' radical monotheism is that idols of all kinds are rejected, though the prophets of course acknowledged the widespread existence of idolatry. They were aware of the subtler forms of spiritual idolatry as well as the more blatant forms of cultic idolatry. In *God and the Attractiveness of Other Paths*, we consider this recurring theme of the prophetic books.

For the prophets the covenant community's relationship with God has priority over all other interests and commitments. However, other interests and commitments are not excluded if they are compatible with covenantal loyalty to God, for it is only within the ordinary activities and relationships of life that faithfulness to God can be understood and fulfilled. But the legitimacy of all interests and commitments is to be evaluated in the light of the covenant.

Israel is God's servant, not the other way around. The implications of this relationship are developed fully only in Isaiah 40–55, but the basic understanding suggested by it is implicit in other prophetic writings as well. According to the prophets, the human attempt to use God to gain advantages in life was one of the prevailing features of Israel's religion, and many forms of this effort are described and assessed in the prophetic writings. The prophets, on the other hand, constantly exhorted Israel to obey God faithfully. The primary covenantal relation is between God and the whole people of Israel. God's relation to the kings and priests is subordinate to this primary relationship. The blessings and moral responsibilities of the covenant are shared by all the people, not merely those in authority. In this sense the leaders have no special status before God but are representative of the people. The prophetic writings presuppose that the kings and priests had special roles in Israel, but the writings judge these leaders on the basis of the fundamental principles of the covenant and not on the grounds of any sanctity inherent in the royal or priestly offices themselves. Social status is not the basis of God's judgment, but righteousness. Kings and priests are judged in the prophetic writings by the same covenantal standards as everyone else. Everyone in the covenant community is equal before God. This presupposition of prophetic thought, and of the tradition of torah which it reflects, is one of the principal sources of Jewish and Christian regard for the worth and dignity of all persons.

Everyone in the covenant community is equally responsible to God to live a life of faithful obedience. This obedience means both being and doing, worship and righteous action, living in right relationship with other persons, and acting as God's covenant partners in maintaining justice. Members of the covenant community are called to overcome injustice, feed the hungry, and care for the orphaned and the widowed. This motif of God's demand for righteousness is mentioned in many of the sermons that appear later in this chapter, and it is the subject of *The Church and the Neediest* in chapter 5.

In text after text the prophets severely criticized Israel's ritual performances and the priests who led them. Some of their evaluations come close to rejecting the cult itself as an instrument of God's grace (e.g., Isa. 1:10-17; Jer. 7:1-17, 21-26; Ezek. 8:1–9:11; Hos. 6:1-6; Amos 5:21-27), but they do not actually repudiate ritual worship as a means of encounter with God. The prophets' criticism of ritual is touched upon in the sermon mentioned above and in the sermon on *The Hierarchy and the Laity*, which is based on the account of Amos's confrontation with Amaziah the priest of Bethel.

Another fundamental conviction underlying the prophetic proclamation is that life in the world is the vital place of our interaction with God. Humans are called to live fully and faithfully in their time and place. The prophets differed from the apocalypticists, whose hope was primarily otherworldly. Even when the prophets spoke about future acts of God or the future conditions of life among the people of God, they did so in this-worldly terms. They believed that God could do new things in the world, but they did not expect God to create a new world, as the apocalypticists did. Nor did they make any assertions about life after death (Isa. 26:19 is the only exception). We are led to suppose that their faith in God was so strong that the question of God's care for people in other lives or other worlds simply never arose. But the prophets spoke eloquently about *God's Providential Care* in the face of future uncertainty in the life of the covenant community. This is the theme of the last sermon in this chapter.

Moral evil—sin—is real, profound, and widespread. Rebellion, apostasy, idolatry, faithlessness, and injustice are the constant themes of the prophets. They say much about the suffering caused by sin but little about the suffering caused by disease or natural disasters. Moreover, the sinfulness that counted for the prophets was not primarily ritual impurity but unrighteousness and injustice in human relations and infidelity to God. Consequently, they showed less interest in ritual means of atonement than in repentance and reformation of life.

The prophets proclaimed God's active working to restore the relationships broken by human conduct. God's grace is creative and redemptive. However, it includes judgment because of the reality of human sin. According to the prophets, redemption often comes only after judgment, particularly the redemption of Israel as a community. God's judgment occurs primarily in the lives of communities and not through natural phenomena, though there are a few allusions to such "acts of God" in the prophetic books (e.g., God's withholding of rain in Amos 4:6-10). But judgment presupposes grace, for one cannot know that it is God's judgment unless one first knows God, which for the covenant community brought into being through God's redemptive acts, means knowing God's grace. God's grace as manifested in forgiveness is the theme of the sermon entitled *God's Reconciling and Healing Grace*.

Because of the depth of human sinfulness, even among the people of God, the prophetic calling can be a costly one, for it includes among other things calling people to account for their moral failures. The prophets were generally unwelcome in the temple, and when they were not ostracized (Amos 7:10-17; Jer. 26), they were ignored (Isa. 6–8). The story of Jeremiah's career contains the fullest exposition of this theme in the prophetic corpus, and a portion of that story is the chosen text in the section entitled *God and the Vocation of Faithful Witness*.

Finally, for the prophets, human beings are unitary. In contemporary terms, we are psychosomatic wholes. In prophetic thought there is no dualism of matter and spirit, of body and soul. The religious question, according to the prophets, is not whether an aspect of human life is spiritual or material, but whether our lives are lived in loving obedience to God. This unity of human life reflects the universal sovereignty of the one God.

This is a brief theological outline of the main elements in the prophetic understanding of God and of human beings before God. Some of these elements are explicit in the prophetic witness, while others are presupposed by it. The discussion that follows is organized around seven themes, but virtually all the themes described above are touched upon in the reflections and sermons that appear here and in chapter 5.

Preaching on Representative Texts

The remainer of this chapter is concerned with the practical task of preaching on major themes of the prophetic witness. We have chosen seven of these themes, and have devoted a separate section to each one. Each section begins with some general reflections on the theme and its bearing on the life of the church today, together with comments on specific prophetic texts in which the theme occurs. These comments are followed by a concise sermon on one particular text. The sermons are meant to be illustrative and not definitive. They are not complete sermons but sermon drafts. When we preach we do not use a manuscript, and these drafts are not verbatim transcripts of the sermons as we have delivered them. They contain the main substance of such sermons, as well as their structure, but they are penultimate drafts and not the "final text." We would each preach them in our own distinctive ways, using introductions and illustrations that are appropriate to the listening congregation in their particular situation and to our own background and experience. The sermons as we have presented them here model possible ways of appropriating the prophetic witness for the Christian witness today. We hope that they will facilitate the task of creating sermons on prophetic texts for other preachers.

A note on the biblical texts. At the beginning of each sermon we quote the text on which the sermon is based. However, in some instances the text is long and only a portion of it is quoted. This is the case, for example, in the first two sermons in this chapter (on Isaiah 40 and the book of Jonah, respectively). In such cases the reader should take care to study the entire text.

1. GOD'S PRESENCE MADE KNOWN IN ISRAEL'S HISTORY

Theological considerations. For the prophets, as for the biblical writers generally, God is known through the community-shaping events of Israel's life among the peoples of the world. Israel's coming into being as a covenantal community in the Mosaic age was the chief outward expression of God's loving presence in its historical pilgrimage. God is known above all as one who hears the cries of the suffering and acts to bring about their liberation and healing. This is the message of the exodus. But God's self-disclosure always creates a bond with those redeemed, a covenant community. This is the message of Sinai. The message of the prophets was shaped by this tradition.

Israel's settlement in the land of Canaan was another gracious act of God, according to covenantal tradition. The prophets presupposed this article of Israel's faith, but they viewed Israel's eventual expulsion from the land as God's punishment for infidelity during the era of the monarchy. After the exile, the prophets interpreted the displacement of Babylon by Persia as a further manifestation of God's redemptive purpose and an opportunity for the renewal of Israel's covenant with God. These were the main events in which the prophets discerned the disclosure of God's righteousness and steadfast love.

Prophetic texts dealing with God's presence in Israel's history. Most of the prophetic oracles from the eighth and seventh centuries deal in one way or another with the decline and fall of the Israelite kingdoms, and most of the later oracles deal with the renewal of the Israelite community after the Babylonian exile. A few oracles treat the whole story of God and Israel. The most concise of these, and one of the best suited for preaching, is Hosea 11. This famous passage not only surveys the principal moments of Israel's history (i.e., the redemption of Israel through the exodus from Egypt, the chastisement of the nation, and later the nation's renewal), but also interprets these moments as manifestations of God's enduring love. This is done under the vivid metaphor of God as Israel's mothering parent. No other prophetic interpretation of Israel's history says so much so well in such brief compass.

Hosea 11 is an eminently preachable text. The presence of the loving God in the creation and reformation of Israel is the encompassing theme of the chapter. Also, the question of how Israel knows God is answered as clearly and memorably as anywhere in the Bible. The climax comes in v. 9 with the assertion that God's love for Israel transcends human love, because God's love does not change even in the face of stubborn rejection.

This same message of God's nurturing presence is presented in Hosea 1–3 and 14. In chapter 14 the prophet speaks of God, not as a parent, but as an evergreen tree giving shade from the sun. This is a strong metaphor, as is that of a lion roaring to the pride in Hosea 11:10, but it does not suggest the same depth and breadth of relationship as the metaphor of God as a mothering parent. Chapters 1–3 are nearly as suggestive in this regard as chapter 11, for they employ the metaphor of God as husband. These chapters are longer and more richly detailed than chapter 11, but they pose problems for preaching. First, they contain several pericopes, each in a different literary form. Second, they employ the metaphor of God as a husband betrayed by an adulterous wife. This usage reinforces the traditional patriarchal bias of much of our religion, as well as the ancient stereotype of women as harlots. Hosea 2 was chosen for a sermon on sexual discrimination in chapter 5, because it illustrates the problems associated with patriarchialism so well.

Many oracles of the pre-exilic prophets deal with God's gracious presence in Israel's history, but the majority of them concentrate on Israel's infidelity to God's love and the dire consequences that occur as a result. The problem with these oracles is not that they are irrelevant to our situation today. Quite the contrary! The problem is that most of them are entirely negative. They describe the human problem vividly, but they do not suggest the means of resolution, as a sermon ought to do. As a result, the preacher must use other texts to affirm God's redemptive love. The link between text and sermon is more direct when the primary text supports the main thesis of the sermon, and the main thesis should be God's gracious redemption. Grace is what Christian preaching is all about. Therefore, a text like Hosea 11 is preferable to an oracle of pure judgment.

Isaiah 40–55 contains many appropriate texts for preaching on the theme of God's presence in history. The opening chapter, which is the text for our first sermon in chapter 5, summarizes the message of God's work and focuses on the responsibility of the Israelite community as witnesses of God's redemption. Chapter 45 contains an equally important word about God's action in history. It declares Cyrus of Persia, the conqueror of the Babylonian Empire, as the messiah of God and the anointed king who serves as the agent of God's justice among the nations, even though Cyrus does not know God. In the other chapters

Israel's historic experience of God is proclaimed as the foundation of its hope and its commitment to the future.

The tone of Isaiah 40–55 is positive, encouraging, consolatory, hopeful, and confident, with little accusation of sin or threat of judgment. These chapters were addressed originally to the remnant of the Jewish community living in Judah after the fall of Jerusalem (587 B.C.E.) and to exiles living in Babylonia. The people were encouraged, after they received permission from the Persian government, to do their part in rebuilding the covenant community and to perform their proper service to God as witnesses among the nations. The prophet's appeal is grounded not only in the historic opportunity facing Israel at the time, but also in the enduring grace of God, whose word stands *forever* (v. 8) and who *always* gives power to the faint (v. 29). Therefore, the relevance of the prophet's message is not limited to the particular circumstances of the exile, but extends to the life of "those who wait for God" (v. 31) in every age.

The structure of the sermon. We have used a problem-resolution-new possibility structure in the following sermon. All three parts are based directly on the text itself: the problem is the people's discouragement ("Our way is hidden from the Lord"); the resolution is the prophet's proclamation of the reality of God as creator and redeemer (The Good News to Zion); and the new possibility is to wait creatively for the revelation of God's glory to all the world ("The glory of the Lord shall be revealed to all people"). Thus, the sermon as a whole is expository of the biblical passage. Proclaiming the reality of God, and the *coming* revelation of God's glory, is the immediate possibility opened to Israel, when it appropriates the prophet's word of God's comfort and empowerment. Israel is called to remember and to proclaim who God is and what God has done. The ultimate outcome is the revelation of God's glory to all people everywhere.

THE REVELATION OF GOD IN ISRAEL'S PILGRIMAGE: A SERMON ON ISAIAH 40

Comfort, O comfort my people, says your God. . . . In the wilderness prepare the way of God, make straight in the desert a highway for our God. . . . The glory of the Lord shall be revealed, and all people shall see it together, for the mouth of God has spoken. . . . All people are grass, their constancy is like the flower of the field . . . but the word of our God will stand forever. . . . Why do you say, O Israel, "My way is hidden from the Lord?" . . . (The Lord) gives power to the faint, and strengthens the powerless. . . . Those who wait for the Lord shall renew their strength, they shall mount up with wings like eagles, they shall run and not be weary, they shall walk and not faint. (Isaiah 40:1-31)

"Our way is hidden from the Lord" [The Problem]

The people of the covenant were deeply discouraged. For three generations after the fall of the kingdom of Judah, Jerusalem and its temple lay in ruins. The Holy City, the symbol and center of David's kingdom, where the disparate tribes of Israel had been united in a common venture under God, was nothing but rubble, a heap of stones. And the sanctuary of God, Solomon's crowning achievement as a builder and the focus of Israel's religious life for four hundred years, was completely gone, leaving the "mountain of God" a bare height—silent and empty. Entire villages were reduced to ashes, their inhabitants dead or in exile. And the descendants of the survivors waited in the ruins, or in far away Babylonia, with failing hope for a change in fortune. Their children, born and reared in an alien land, had never seen Jerusalem or the temple of God, and knew nothing of the ancient ways of covenantal life. The great festivals of the past were memories of their grandparents, dimly imagined and unreal. What was real to them was the life in Babylon, rich, varied, and alluring. Like the youth of today, they were disenchanted with their parents' religion and fascinated by the vibrant culture around them. For many of their parents, the destruction of Jerusalem and the temple was proof of God's weakness, and they, too, turned to other gods. Those who were left wondered whether the God of their ancestors was still present among them.

To understand the people's discouragement we need only recall our own worst experiences of loss and bereavement. The loss of a beloved child or spouse, the loss of a career and the dreams of a lifetime, or the loss of our health or our home. Now try to imagine the loss of a community, a culture, a way of life. The people of Israel had lost everything, and their discouragement with God was complete. They had lost their vocation as the people of God.

God had revealed Godself to the community in the past. God had been present in the experiences of the ancestors, such as Abraham and Sarah, or Isaac and Rebekah, leading them in the journey of their lives. God had been present in the liberation of the exodus and the wandering in the wilderness, in the giving of the covenant at Sinai, in the settlement in the promised land and the formation of the nation. But where was God now? Where was God in the midst of the ruins: ruined homes, ruined nation, ruined hopes? Israel's way was hidden from the eyes of God, for God was no longer present. God did not know the people any longer, and they did not know God.

The Good News to Zion [The Resolution]

But the revelation of God is not just a thing of the past. It takes place here and now in the present. It comes to the discouraged remnant of Israel through the voice of the messenger, the herald of good news to Zion. God is present in the midst of the people through the words of the prophet. God is at hand, "Comfort, comfort my people" (Isa. 40:1).

What kind of comfort is the prophet offering? The comfort of God's gracious presence, of course. But it is not simply the drying of their tears. It is more than a balm for their wounded spirits. The comfort of which the prophet speaks is a revitalization, an empowerment, a rejuvenation. The comforted will "renew their strength;" "they will mount up with wings like eagles;" "they shall run and not be weary." And the prophet's word is so empowering because it is the word about who God is.

Who is God? Whose word does the prophet proclaim? This was the fundamental question for the ancient Jewish exiles, and it is fundamental for us, too. It is the most serious question of all, for everything we think and do is affected by our answer to it. Who we are and who we can become depends upon our understanding of who God is. Our faith shapes our being, as it shapes our behavior.

The answer the prophet gives to the question—Who is God?—is, God is the creator of the ends of the earth, who gives life and strength to everything that lives, who outlasts the rise and fall of kingdoms, and who is the ultimate guide and arbiter of human destiny. God is the unifying purpose beneath the vast diversity of things in nature and the myriad events of history. The one whom the prophet summons Israel to trust and to proclaim is the ultimate source and end of all things. Any other object of devotion is an idol and not God. There is nothing in the world, nothing at all, worthy of ultimate devotion or capable of bestowing lasting value upon our lives. Even the greatest nations are short-lived, and the gods of those nations are equally finite and ephemeral. There is nothing in the world that is worthy of our ultimate devotion. Yet idolatry of one kind or another is universal. Idolatry is a daily human temptation to which we all succumb. The question about who God is, then, is urgent.

The prophet addresses this profound human question. It is not surprising that exiled Israel, whose importance was completely negated, not only by the enormity of the cosmos but also by the events of history, should declare, "My way is hidden from the Lord!" (40:27). But amazingly the prophet replies that God, the creator of all things, not only knows Israel's way but cares about its people (40:29-31). The creator loves and sustains every one of the people, from the ones that are exhausted and discouraged all the way down to the weariest of trudgers. God knows each one's need, cares about it, and satisfies it. And all that we must do is to "wait" for God, that is, to trust God steadfastly. Our way is not hidden from God. On the contrary, God is with us in every moment, sharing in our pain and sorrow, loving us, and seeking our love in return. God's love is at work among us, to bring about peace, joy, and fulfillment.

The prophetic word of comfort reaffirms the reality of the one true God and reassures the people of God's empowering presence in the midst of life. And this word of comfort comes with a promise for the future. This promise is directed beyond the immediate needs of the discouraged people, and it reminds them of their place in God's plan. The promise is not just for this discouraged flock of exiles or even for the nation of Israel. The promise is for the whole world: The glory of the Lord shall be revealed to all people. One day, everyone, everywhere will know that the whole of life is interconnected in God's love.

"The glory of the Lord shall be revealed to all people" [The New Possibility]

But the future is not yet here. The people in Isaiah's congregation had to wait. Indeed, we, too, are still waiting for the world to know the glory of the Lord. But our waiting, like that of ancient Israel, is not passive. We are strengthened, renewed, revitalized for a mission. The prophet uses the metaphor of "highway construction" to speak of how the people of God should wait in faith. He summons the faithful to prepare a highway through the desert, built over mountains that have been leveled and through valleys that have been filled in. It is an international highway from Babylon to Jerusalem! This is a metaphor that everyone who uses interstate highways can understand at once. Highways require planning, an enormous amount of labor, and are very costly. They need constant maintenance. But highways are absolutely necessary if people are going to travel anywhere and accomplish their goals. The point of the prophet's metaphor is that we are God's co-creators, and we, too, must work if God's glory is to be seen by all peoples.

Israel is reminded of its place in God's providential plan. The prophet Isaiah had declared two hundred years earlier, in his famous vision of God enthroned in the temple, that the whole earth was filled with God's glory. Now another prophet declares that God's glory will be revealed to all people. God's glory is for everyone to see. For that to occur there must be heralds of the good news. There must be preachers of God's word. Responsibility for proclaiming this word is shared by every member of the community, a responsibility transmitted from the prophet to his faltering congregation, and from them to the rest of Zion and out to all the cities of Judah, and beyond to the ends of the earth. The preached word enables eyes of flesh to perceive the glory of God. God's glory, and God's loving, forgiving, and sustaining presence are not revealed to the world without the word of witness. Through the word of witness God's presence comes again and again to the covenant community and to all people everywhere. It is this word about the living God, the creator of heaven and earth, the one who forgives, comforts, and sustains us along our path, that we are called upon to share with everyone in the world.

2. THE BOUNDARIES OF GOD'S LOVE

Boundaries mark the limits within which we live our lives. Some boundaries are set by nature. These are not too difficult to identify and understand. Human beings cannot fly. We must eat, sleep, and exercise to remain healthy. If we pollute the natural environment and deplete its resources, it will no longer support life. Other boundaries involve human relationships. These, too, mark the limits within which we live our lives, but they are not as easily identified and understood as the natural boundaries. There are boundaries defining our personal property and the property of nations. There are boundaries defining our citizenship, and our membership in various groups. And there are boundaries that identify the type of behavior that is acceptable in various kinds of relationships.

People have always struggled with boundaries of this second category, relational boundaries. But some relational boundaries are particularly controversial today in this era of great social change. Many social boundaries that were accepted in the past have been exposed as unfair and have been changed to enable more people to live fuller, freer lives. Yet this changing of traditional boundaries can be unsettling. We resist it if it means instability, and yearn for the security of traditional boundaries.

Boundaries become a religious issue when we claim that the communal or cultural boundaries that we have created are God's boundaries. It is particularly tempting to make this claim in the covenant community, because the covenant community has a distinctive vocation in the larger community. Boundaries of action and association which may be entirely cultural in origin can be rationalized as expressions of God's will, with the result that these boundaries serve to limit God's love.

The Israelites experienced God's love in the great community-forming acts of covenantal history, and they regulated their life in conformity to God's will, as they were able to discern it. Those who did not live accordingly were thought to be beyond the bounds of God's blessing, outside the limits of God's grace, while those who did were tempted to take pride in their moral superiority and to take comfort in their special access to God. The prophets challenged this understanding of the boundaries of God's love. They did not deny that disobedience of God's will had destructive effects. On the contrary, they spoke constantly of such effects as the judgments of God. But they did deny Israel's pretensions in relation to other peoples. Amos affirmed that God's providential guidance of Israel was not different from God's guidance of the Ethiopians (Amos 9:7). Jeremiah affirmed that the well-being (*shalom*) of the Jewish exiles in Babylonia was tied up with that of the Babylonians, on whose behalf the exiles should pray to God (Jer. 29:1-14). The writer of Isaiah 19:19-25 proclaimed God's equal care for Assyrians and Egyptians, along with the Israelites. And the writer of the book of Jonah captured this witness to the universality of God's love in an unforgettable story.

The structure of the sermon. Because the book of Jonah is a short story, the most straightforward structure to use in preaching on it is to retell the story. As it happens, the story has a problem-resolution-new possbility structure, though in this case the possibility is only partly stated. The first part presents the problem (*Jonah resists God's call*); the second, the resolution (*God Persists in Calling Jonah*); and the third, the new possibility (*The Question for Jonah and for Us*). The possibility for the Ninevites is described: they repent when Jonah preaches to them, and are reconciled to God. The possibility for Jonah is to affirm God's grace and become more compassionate. The book ends with God's question to him, which Jonah has not yet answered for himself. Accordingly, the sermon ends with an open question to the congregation.

GOD'S UNBOUNDED LOVE: A SERMON ON THE BOOK OF JONAH

> Now the word of God came to Jonah son of Amittai saying, "Go at once to Nineveh, that great city, and cry out against it; for their wickedness has come up before me." But Jonah set out to flee to Tarshish from the presence of God. . . . The word of God came to Jonah a second time, saying, "Get up, go to Nineveh, that great city, and proclaim to it the message that I tell you." So Jonah set out and went to Nineveh . . . and cried out . . . and the people of Nineveh believed God. . . . But this was very displeasing to Jonah, and he became angry. . . . And God said to Jonah, . . . "Should I not be concerned about Nineveh, that great city, in which there are more than a hundred and twenty thousand persons who do not know their right hand from their left, and also many animals?" (Jonah 1:1-3; 3:1-5; 4:1-11)

Jonah Resists God's Call [The Problem]

The book of Jonah tells the story of a prophet who resists obeying the call of God, and of a God who works even through a resentful messenger to accomplish God's gracious purpose. The story is a parable about the community of faith, a parable about ourselves.

God commands Jonah to go to Nineveh and warn the city that God's judgment is coming, but Jonah takes a ship in the opposite direction and tries to hide from God. However, God finds him out and by means of a terrible storm at sea, some newly converted sailors, and a large, obedient fish, God fetches Jonah back. The sea and the storm obey the voice of God, the sailors obey, and the fish obeys, but Jonah does not obey. Once again God commands him to go preach to Nineveh, and this time Jonah, worn down, goes as he is commanded.

Jonah makes the long trek to Nineveh and goes right to the center of the vast city. He cries out just five words: "In forty days Nineveh's doomed!" (author translation). His mission completed, Jonah goes out and sits down on a hill overlooking the city, and waits to see what will happen. Hearing the terrible news that Jonah has broadcast to the city, the king and people all repent. They declare their faith in God and perform acts of penitence, and the gracious God relents from judgment. Thus the Ninevite people are saved. But Jonah is so furious that he wants to die, and at last he reveals the reason why he did not want to obey God's command, "O Lord, isn't this what I said while I was still in my country? That is why I fled to Tarshish at the beginning; for I knew that you are a gracious God and merciful, slow to anger, and abounding in steadfast love, and ready to relent from punishing. So now, O Lord, take my life from me!" (4:2-3).

Jonah has known all along that God is a loving and merciful God, who forgives and redeems penitent sinners. He knows that God's love is not limited by political boundaries or the enmities of nations. But Jonah is angry that God loves without boundaries. And so, in misery, under a burning Assyrian sun, Jonah takes comfort from the shade of a leafy vine that grows up suddenly over him. And then, just as suddenly, the vine is killed by a voracious worm. Jonah is so furious at the death of the wonderful vine that once again he wants to die. The story ends when God observes Jonah's fury over the salvation of Nineveh and his fury over the death of the vine, and God asks Jonah, who has shown compassion for the vine, whether God did not do right by showing compassion to Nineveh. God's question is not answered. As far as we know, Jonah is still furious at the end, and the question is left for each of us to answer for ourselves.

There are many reasons why members of the community of faith resist the call of God, and most of these we can appreciate. Jeremiah struggled with his call because he felt inadequate. Sarah doubted her call to bear a child because of her advanced age and her lifelong barrenness. Moses resisted God's call because of the enormity of the task. The list could go on. Jonah, however, does not resist his call because of discouragement, or failure to trust God's grace, or mere pig-headedness. He resists because he detests the Ninevites and wants them destroyed. Jonah knows the reality of God's grace and mercy, "You are a gracious God and merciful, slow to anger, and abounding in steadfast love" (4:2). But the Ninevites are an alien people who ruled Israel for a long time; and Jonah refuses to accept his appointment to be a means of their salvation. He resists God's call to ministry, because he refuses to be an instrument of God's love for people he despises. Unlike Jeremiah, Sarah, and Moses,

Jonah does not doubt his ability as a servant of God, or God's power to work through him. His problem is just the opposite. He knows God's power and mercy, and he rejects God's purpose in calling him to serve. Jonah wants to limit the boundaries of God's love.

God Persists in Calling Jonah [The Resolution]

God deals with Jonah's refusal by wearing him down, until Jonah finally obeys God's command. No matter which way Jonah turns, no matter what he does to hide from God, God pursues him, hounding him to obey his prophetic calling, and to grow more compassionate in the process.

Jonah must choose whether he will share in the divine compassion or try to limit God's love. We understand Jonah's reluctance. We understand the prophet's anger over God's concern for godless and unjust people. It is very difficult to have compassion for such people, especially when they are our enemies. Like Jonah, we can reject the claim that God's love places over our lives—the call to love God and everyone whom God loves, including our enemies—but like Jonah, we cannot escape from God. We cannot flee from God's presence. Grace surrounds us, every moment of every day, wherever we may be. The mystery of the relationship of grace and human will is that we have the freedom to reject the call of God. Nevertheless, God's searching love pursues us until we choose to become co-workers with God, and thus to become the men and women God has created us to be.

Jonah obeyed God, but Jonah was not reconciled to God. This was the heart of Jonah's problem. And, being unreconciled to God, it was impossible for him to be reconciled to his enemies, the Ninevites, even after they repented of their wickedness and confessed their faith in God. On one level the story of Jonah is a story of God's compassion for Nineveh. The story ends with the poignant question, unanswered in Jonah's heart: Was God right to show mercy to the repentant city? On another level the story is about God's compassion for Jonah. In his own way Jonah is also an enemy of God, for he does not share God's love for all God's creatures, and he does not live and act out of such love. So Jonah's deepest problem is his alienation from God, from the God of love, whose love claims our love even as it is offered to us as a gift. God's resolution of this problem is to appeal to Jonah to be reconciled to God's love.

The Question for Jonah and for Us [The New Possibility]

Why does God's love encompass those we cannot love, the torturers, the rapists, the plunderers of this world, the people who have cheated and abused us and violated the lives of innocent, helpless people? In the story, God tries to help Jonah come to terms with this question through the parable of the vine. When Jonah protests bitterly over the loss of the ruined vine, which has served his needs very well, God offers him an unperturbed reply, and this reply makes clear who sets the boundaries of God's love. Jonah is angry because of the plant, but it is God's plant. Jonah has not worked for it; it is God's gift. Jonah has not created it, and its final destiny lies in God's hands, not Jonah's. And so it is with Nineveh. Its people and its animals are God's, not Jonah's. "Should I not be concerned for Nineveh, that great city . . . and all those animals?" (author translation). God's tone to the resentful prophet is calm, but the meaning is unsettling, for it challenges the impulses of Jonah's heart and his deep loyalty to his own people, people who have suffered terribly at the hands of the Ninevites.

God cares about the covenant community and all its members. But we have no special position of privilege in the world. God is the God of heaven and earth, of all things living and dead. Grace encompasses all people; God's compassion for sinners knows no bounds. However, the community of faith has a special position of responsiblity in the human community. It is called to bear witness to God through its works of love, and like Jonah, through its prophetic preaching. It bears the message of grace so that all may hear and turn to the God whose love enfolds all life. God cares about Nineveh, with its masses of confused people and its herds of animals, just as God cares about the whole world, simply because it is there. That is unconditional care—pure, unbounded love—which seeks the repentance, the restoration and fulfillment of all, no matter how wicked they may be.

The possibilities opened to Jonah are either joyful acceptance of the wide boundaries of God's love or grudging resistance. Will Jonah accept the gift and demand of grace in the end, or will he continue to cry that he would rather be dead? God sets the boundaries of God's love, not we. We are given the gift of grace freely; will we accept its radical challenge to our pride and our preconceptions? Will we bear witness unto the ends of the earth, even to our most hated enemies? Or will we continue to find it easier to preach the message of God's radical, all-compassionate love to those who are already lovable? Jonah never learns to like the Ninevites or to find satisfaction in what God has called him to do. In the story, Jonah's heart never catches up with his decision to obey. He remains reluctant; he still hates Nineveh. Since he is not reconciled to his fellow human beings, people whom God loves, he is not fully reconciled to God. Thus, when the story ends there is still room for Jonah to grow in compassion, to be reconciled to God's love. He has done what he was called to do, but his struggle with God is not over. We know what happened to Nineveh, but we are left not knowing what happened to Jonah. The story is unfinished, leaving us with an unanswered question. If the story is about the Jonah in each of us, it leaves us all to answer the unanswered question for ourselves. Did God do right in showing compassion to Nineveh, that great city with more than a hundred twenty thousand people, who did not know their right hand from their left, and the many animals that also lived there? And if God did right, can we share God's unbounded love?

3. GOD'S RECONCILING AND HEALING GRACE

If God's grace working through judgment is the primary theme of the pre-exilic prophetic oracles, the primary theme of the post-exilic oracles is God's grace working through mercy and redemption. Grace is certainly not absent from the witness of the pre-exilic prophets, for their entire message presupposes the grace of God as the basis of covenantal life. Furthermore, several of the pre-exilic prophets, notably Isaiah and Hosea, expressed confidence in the eventual renewal of the Israelite community through the active working of God's grace. But it was in the time of Israel's greatest suffering and despair, during the exile, that the prophets turned to the task of encouraging and healing their people, and reaffirmed the redemptive love of God, which had always been the underlying foundation of their witness of faith.

Isaiah 2:1-4 is the first text we encounter in the prophetic canon on the theme of God's reconciling and healing grace. It prophesies the eventual reconciliation of all nations as a result of the teaching of God's Torah, and the elimination of war as a mode of interaction. Isaiah 6 describes Isaiah's experience of reconciliation and healing through the forgiveness of Isaiah's sinfulness, and points to the possibility of Israel's eventual reconciliation through the chastening fire of God's judgment. Isaiah 11 depicts the ideal leader of God's people, who is imbued with the Spirit of God. This charismatic leader is able to discern and implement the truth. He judges people as they really are, not as they appear, and he maintains justice for the poor and weak. The fruit of his leadership is reconciliation among the creatures of the world, both human and non-human. Jeremiah's complaints (e.g., Jer. 11:18–12:6) chronicle his experience of alienation from God, resulting from his persecution as a prophet, and his experience of reconciliation, resulting from his assurance of God's sustaining grace.

Our chosen text is Ezekiel 18, a discourse about guilt and forgiveness, in the form of a parable. The point of the discourse is pastoral as well as theological. It is meant to clarify the relationship between God and the covenant people, as well as to provide practical guidance to the people in exile. Ezekiel regards the fall of the Judean kingdom as final, and holds out no hope of its restoration. The past is dead, though the remnant of despairing and bitter people of Judah are not. For the prophet there is no going back to the way things were nor any questioning of God's just treatment of the community. But he affirms that it is possible to be free, before God, from the crippling weight of the past and to live righteously and faithfully in the present.

The text deals with two related questions, both of which have deep existential significance for the people of God. The first asks about the responsibility of the individual before God at a moment of extreme hardship for the community. Are people free to live their lives responsibly before God in the present, or must they be bound forever to suffer because of what has been done in the past, by themselves and others? The second question is one of God's justice, which is often raised by the people of God when they are despairing. During the exilic period, the future of the covenant community was in doubt, and the ancient Israelites questioned the divine justice.

The structure of the sermon. The sermon is constructed according to the problem-resolution-new possibility paradigm, which is particularly appropriate for this text. The people's complaint, which is the occasion for Ezekiel's parable, is quoted and explained (*The Burden of the Past*). This states the problem. Next Ezekiel's response to the complaint is described (*The Prophet's Parable*). The parable presents the resolution of the problem, namely God's demand for righteousness and willingness to forgive the repentant sinner. In addition it points to the new possibility which is affirmed in the third part of the sermon (*God's Ways are not Our Ways)* and is reinforced with a memorable quotation from Isaiah 55.

THE GIFT AND CLAIM OF GOD'S GRACE: A SERMON ON EZEKIEL 18

The word of God came to me: What do you mean by repeating this proverb concerning the land of Israel, "The parents have eaten sour grapes, and the children's teeth are set on edge"? As I live, says the Lord God, this proverb shall no more be used by you in Israel. Know that all lives are mine, the life of the parent as well as the life of the child: it is only the person who sins that shall die. . . . Cast away from you all the transgressions that you have committed against me, and get yourselves a new heart and a new spirit! Why will you die, O house of Israel? For I have no pleasure in the death of anyone, says the Lord God. Turn, then, and live. (Ezekiel 18:1-32)

The Burden of the Past [The Problem]

The Bible acknowledges the powerful and destructive forces that seem to control our destiny and curtail our capacity to shape our own lives. Yet the Bible also affirms our moral freedom and God's claim over our lives in times of narrow confinement as well as in times of unlimited horizons. It is easy to lose sight of our freedom and to become convinced that we have no moral responsibility in the present, restricted moment, when we seem to have little control over our lives.

Pre-exilic prophets like Amos castigate the powerful and privileged in Israel. But Ezekiel proclaims his message to Jews actually living in exile in Babylon. They are questioning the ground rules of the covenant, the terms set by God for living in right relationship with God, and with one another as a holy people. The exiles are descendants of the covenant community who were deported from their homes and their country by Babylonian conquerors. They have suffered under a bondage that began in their parents' generation, and they express their feelings in a memorable proverb: "The parents have eaten sour grapes and the children's teeth are set on edge." In other words, *we* are suffering for what our parents have done and experienced!

The exiles' complaint was correct in large part. If ever a younger generation had cause to blame their parents for their predicament, it was the exiles in Ezekiel's time, living out their lives in bondage and shame. Yet, the same thing is true of those of us who live on the fringes of society today, the poor, the uneducated, the victims of racial injustice and sexual discrimination. We, too, know what it is like to suffer for the sins of previous generations, and we, too, are tempted to become embittered victims, despairing of our freedom to exercise genuine responsiblity for our lives. Individually and corporately we experience the effects of our parents' failures and the failures of past generations. Our ancestors have eaten sour grapes, and our teeth are set on edge. We despair and wonder whether God is fair.

The Prophet's Parable [The Resolution]

Ezekiel responds to the exiles' bitter proverb by telling a parable about sin and family relationships. The characters are a father, a son, and a grandson, but they could also be a mother, a daughter, and a granddaughter. In this family, the father sins, but the son, who is righteous, does not die because of his father's sin. Instead he lives because of his own righteousness. And the grandson, who sins like his grandfather, does not live because of his father's righteousness, but dies because of his sin—not his grandfather's, but his own. But, Ezekiel insists, if the grandfather and grandson turn from their unrighteousness, they will live, and if the father turns from his righteousness, he will die. Living faithfully is not an irreversible action nor is living unfaithfully. In either case we can reverse the direction of our life!

Ezekiel uses the metaphors of *living* and *dying* to speak of the way of life a person chooses before God, and in relationship with others in the covenant community. We die when we fail to be the persons God intends us to be at the heart of our being. And this dying wreaks havoc in the web of relationships in which we live—in our family, the covenant community, the political order, and the natural world. Correspondingly, the life the righteous receive from God is deeply personal, beginning with a transformation of the heart. And it, too, is embodied in all our relationships.

Ezekiel's message was not what the exiles wanted to hear. They had every reason to be bitter about their circumstances. They sought a speedy return to Jerusalem and a renewal of their former way of life. They wanted God to give them back the kingdom and to restore everything they had lost. What is more, they were not at all pleased with God. If anyone deserved a break it was the people who had suffered through no fault of their own, and it seemed as if God would not provide one for them.

Now Ezekiel did not say a word about the responsibility of the privileged in society to relieve the pain of the suffering! That is another issue. Nor did he say anything about our responsiblity to do all we can to change oppressive structures that restrict the paths open to us! That, too, is another issue. Ezekiel's word is simply about our responsiblity before God, and God's right to decide how to judge us. God chooses to judge each of us according to our ways.

God's Ways Are Not Our Ways [The New Possibility]

Are God's ways just? Should God judge us by our ways in the present moment, and not by our circumstances, or by what our parents have done, or by what we ourselves have done in the past? Ezekiel's answer to the people's questioning of the fairness of God's ways is to turn the question back on the people: Thus says the Lord, "O house of Israel, are my ways not just? Is it not your ways that are not just?" (author translation). Ezekiel will not let the people question the righteousness of God. His answer focuses on the faithfulness of the people in the present, not on what their parents have done in the past. The people could not recover the past, erase its bitter tragedies, or reclaim its joy and security. They had to leave the past in God's hand. Like us, they could live faithfully only in the here and now, by the grace that is given to us in the present moment. The question for us, too, is not whether God's ways are just, but whether our ways are just.

It is not easy to appropriate Ezekiel's counsel, expecially when we feel paralyzed by wounds inflicted by our parents and by society. Ezekiel's answer is that the grace of God is not limited by the dead weight of the past, nor is our freedom to respond to grace destroyed. We are beings who have the freedom to choose who we are today and what we will be tomorrow, despite what others have done in the past or the mistakes we ourselves have made. It is true that our teeth are set on edge by the sour grapes our parents have eaten, but our life before God is determined by our own decision to live in grateful response to God's love, or to turn away from that love. That is the logic of Ezekiel's parable.

The counsel of the prophet Ezekiel stood the test of time. Two generations later, the dispersed survivors of the house of Israel were free to return to their homeland after bitter exile in Babylonia and Egypt. The prophet Isaiah celebrated this time of redemption with a hymn of praise for the mystery of God's grace to Israel. Hear Isaiah's words, which echo the truth and wisdom of Ezekiel:

> Seek the Lord while he may be found, call upon him while he is near; let the wicked forsake their way, and the unrighteous their thoughts; let them return to the Lord, that he may have mercy on them, and to our God, for he will abundantly pardon. For my

thoughts are not your thoughts, nor are your ways my ways, says
the Lord. For as the heavens are higher than the earth, so are my
ways higher than your ways and my thoughts than your thoughts.
For as the rain and the snow come down from heaven, and do
not return there until they have watered the earth, making it
bring forth and sprout, giving seed to the sower and bread to the
eater, so shall my word be that goes forth from my mouth; it shall
not return to me empty, but it shall accomplish that which I
purpose, and succeed in the thing for which I sent it. (Isaiah
55:6-11)

4. GOD AND THE VOCATION OF FAITHFUL WITNESS

The prophets were scorned and persecuted for their candor.
Amos was expelled from the national sanctuary in Bethel (Amos
7:10-17), Isaiah's counsel to Ahaz was rejected (Isa. 6–8), and
Jeremiah's life was threatened (Jer. 26; 37-38). The painful
mission of the prophet of God to unheeding people is classically
depicted in Second Isaiah's suffering servant of the Lord (Isa.
42:1-4; 49:1-6; 50:4-9; 52:13–53:12). These servant songs, as they
are called, have been prominent in Christian usage because of
their obvious parallels to Jesus' life. The biblical story of Jeremiah merits our attention, too, for it is an extraordinary story
of candor and faith in the midst of prolonged personal suffering
for one's religious vocation.

The text selected for our sermon is Jeremiah 15:15-21. It is
one of a series of complaints—or laments, as they are often
called—addressed to God, in response to the rejection and
persecution suffered by Jeremiah at the hands of the religious
and political leaders of Judah. The other complaints appear in
11:18–12:6, 17:14-18, 18:18-23, and 20:7-18.

There are several points to keep in mind when preaching
from this text. First, there is no "happy ending" to Jeremiah's
story. Public mistreatment persisted to the end of his ministry
(see Jer. 44). Second, there are many causes of inner anguish for
those called by God to ministry. Jonah's anguish, for example,
was caused by his own rebellion against God. The exiles to
whom Ezekiel prophesied were embittered by the destruction
of Judah, which they blamed on the previous generation. Jere-

miah's suffering was particularly poignant, for it was caused by persecution at the hands of the covenant community.

The preacher should bear in mind that prophetic vocation belongs not only to the repesentative, or ordained, ministers but to all ministers of the church, perhaps especially to the laity. Any faithful servant of the word of God can experience wounds like Jeremiah's, which shake the foundations of faith. Jeremiah's anger at God when he felt betrayed is not alien to us. Nor is his desire for God to avenge him on his enemies. Therefore, Jeremiah's prayer can be properly interpreted as the prayer of lament of the whole people of God. Our sermon addresses the pain experienced by all Christians as we seek to be faithful in our vocations.

The structure of the sermon. Here again the structure follows the problem-resolution-new possibility paradigm. At the same time, the sermon tells the story of Jeremiah's failure and rejection as a prophet. Much of this story is gathered from other parts of the book, especially chapter 1 (Jeremiah's call), chapter 26 (his initial rejection), and related chapters. The gist of the story is as follows: Jeremiah was sure of his call to prophecy and of the reality of God. Therefore, when he failed in his mission and was rejected and persecuted for it, he became furious at God. God's response led Jeremiah to reassess and renew his vocational commitment. The new possibility for Jeremiah was that, although his rejection by the people continued, he should keep right on doing what he was called by God to do, bearing witness to God's grace, manifest in judgment and mercy. How much of the story one should tell in a sermon is a question each individual preacher must answer.

GOD'S CALL TO FAITHFUL WITNESS: A SERMON ON JEREMIAH 15

O God . . . in your forbearance do not take me away; know that on your account I suffer insult, . . . for I am called by your name, O Lord, God of hosts. Why is my pain unceasing, my wound incurable, refusing to be healed? Truly, you are to me like a deceitful brook, like waters that fail. Therefore, thus says the Lord: If you turn back, I will take you back, and you shall stand before me. If you utter what is precious, and not what is worth-less, you shall serve as my mouth. (Jer. 15:15-19)

Jeremiah's Anger at God [The Problem]

At some time and place in our journey of faith, most of us have had the experience of being so devasted that our faith begins to crumble. We must struggle to believe that God is a loving God and that life is worthwhile. Those of us who have not yet encountered this kind of faith-shattering experience have either been fortunate or have not lived long enough.

Many kinds of events can challenge our faith—an accident that takes the life of a loved one, the loss of a job that threatens our family's security, or perhaps a crippling disease. But there is a special kind of wound that attacks our heart and mind. It is a betrayal by someone we trust. The pain of betrayal is deep and lasting. It afflicts our souls and erodes our sense of trust, even our trust in God. It is hard to recover from such a wound. It requires an act of faith. The prophet Jeremiah experienced the deep pain of betrayal, and his response can illuminate our journey of faith.

Jeremiah was God's messenger during the last decades of the kingdom of Judah. He had not chosen his vocation, rather God had chosen him. Jeremiah's call to be a prophet was exactly the kind of call that prophets appointed by God had experienced since the days of Moses. Jeremiah recorded his call for us:

> Now the word of the Lord came to me saying, "Before I formed you in the womb I knew you, and before you were born I consecrated you; I appointed you a prophet to the nations." (1:4-5)

Just as the reality of his call was unmistakable, so was his reluctance to be a prophet:

> Then I said, "Ah, Lord God! Truly I do not know how to speak, for I am only a boy." But the Lord said to me, "Do not say, 'I am only a boy'; for you shall go to all to whom I send you, and you shall speak whatever I command you. Do not be afraid of them, for I am with you to deliver you." (1:6-8)

Jeremiah believed that God would support him in his ministry, and because of this assurance, he entrusted himself to God. He proclaimed the fall of Jerusalem and the kingdom of Judah and called Israel to return from its apostasy to the one true God, "the fountain of living water" (Jer. 2:13). Devoted to the covenant people, Jeremiah's preaching was filled with compassion at the devastation inflicted upon Israel:

> For the hurt of my poor people I am hurt, I mourn, and dismay has taken hold on me. Is there no balm in Gilead? Is there no physican there? . . . O that my head were a spring of water, and my eyes a fountain of tears, that I might weep day and night for the slain of my poor people! (8:21–9:1)

But his vocation did not unfold in the way he expected. Everything he did turned sour. His witness to God's righteousness was rebuffed and scorned. He was rejected by the community and treated violently. Nothing came of his preaching except hatred and scorn, even from his own family. His fellow citizens plotted to assassinate him (Jer. 12:18-19), and his life was threatened repeatedly (Jer. 26; 37-38).

His persecutors were not foreign rulers, like the pharaoh of Egypt or the king of Babylon. They were members of the covenant community, people whom Jeremiah trusted and with whom he shared the life of faith, and they betrayed him. Jeremiah reacted to rejection and failure in the same way that we would. Feeling all alone in a hateful universe, he was plagued by doubt. He lost all confidence in himself, all trust in God, all joy in life:

> Cursed be the day on which I was born! The day when my mother bore me! . . . Why did I come forth from the womb to see toil and sorrow, and spend my days in shame? (20:13-18)

Many of us in a similar situation doubt the reality of God. But Jeremiah did not do this. Nor did he doubt the reality of his call to prophecy. God had called him to be a prophet, and the message he proclaimed was surely the word of God (Jer. 15:16)! Jeremiah had been faithful to this call. So why had he failed so miserably? Why had suffering and shame been his lot? God must have misled him when God assured him of support in his vocation (Jer. 1:17-19).

Jeremiah did something astonishing in the midst of his pain. He turned to God with a brutal prayer: "O Lord, you know; remember me and visit me, and bring down retribution for me on my persecutors. . . . Why is my pain unceasing, my wound incurable, refusing to be healed? Truly, you are to me like a deceitful brook, like waters that fail" (15:15-18). Jeremiah pleaded for vengeance against his persecutors, and he hurled a charge of unfaithfulness directly at God, "You have enticed me, and I was enticed!" (20:7).

How many of us have the courage to rage at God when our faithful witness brings us rejection and suffering? The temptation is to turn away from God in bitterness, abandon our vocation, and drift away from the covenant community.

God Answers Jeremiah's Prayer [The Resolution]

Jeremiah's outrage and anger did not go unanswered. Through the inner voice of his self-searching, God's answer came to him. First of all he heard the summons to repent and entrust himself once more to God, in spite of what had happened. Then he realized that to accuse God of deceiving him was to utter something "worthless." God was not responsible for his plight; it arose from the deep conflict between his message of judgment and the desires of the Judean people. Suffering in his vocation was not God's fault but the consequence of human sin. God did not cause Jeremiah's suffering but shared his suffering with him. In Jeremiah's rejection, God was rejected too.

Jeremiah received no assurance that God would avenge him against those who had abused him unjustly. He had pleaded with God, "Let my persecutors be shamed, but do not let me be shamed; let them be dismayed, but do not let me be dismayed; bring on them the day of disaster; destroy them with double destruction!" (17:18). Surely Jeremiah was right in confessing his deep yearning for vengeance to God. But his prayer for vengeance was answered in a way he did not expect. He heard God telling him that if he was to act truly as the mouth of God, he must not imitate his persecutors, but should let them imitate him, "It is they who will turn to you, not you who will turn to them" (15:19); or, to paraphrase the text, "Do not descend to their level, let them rise to yours."

God's response to Jeremiah's bitter prayer ends with a promise. If Jeremiah will go on faithfully to bear his prophetic witness, God will not abandon him. He may not win the praise of other people, but he will never be alone. He will know that God is with him, strengthening him, "They will fight against you, but they shall not prevail over you, for I am with you to save and deliver you, says the Lord. I will deliver you out of the hand of the wicked, and redeem you from the grasp of the ruthless" (15:20-21).

Deeper Understanding, Stronger Faith [The New Possibility]

Jeremiah's bold protest to God not only brought him inner assurance but it deepened his theological discernment. He gained greater clarity about his relationship with God in the unfolding events of his life, and as a result he reassessd his relationship with the people of Judah who had rejected him. Jeremiah's need for personal vengeance fell away, and he became once more a channel for the word of God. God's word was a word of judgment for the kingdom of Judah in Jeremiah's time, to be sure, but it was *God's* judgment and not Jeremiah's. Jeremiah's vindication rested entirely in God's hands and not in any retaliation of his own. He was set free from the terrible burden of revenge, set free to fulfill his vocation within the community of the covenant, to be the prophet that God intended him to be.

When our journeys of faith fail to bring the results we expect, when we encounter betrayal, suffering, and loss, we may be puzzled and uncertain of our calling as people of faith. When the pain is unceasing we are tempted in three ways: (1) to become angry at God, (2) to feel vengeful toward those who have injured us, and (3) to doubt ourselves and perhaps to despair. But when God's word comes to us, it challenges us to turn away from these temptations and trust God again. God sends us back again and again to bear witness to the gift and claim of God's love by our words and our deeds. God is neither a deceiver nor the cause of our suffering. God shares in our works of love and in the pain we may suffer for them. But God does not smooth the path for us, or remove the obstacles, or guarantee the results we want. God sends us back to be faithful in our calling and to invite others to share in this same calling, with all its potential for pain, but with the assurance of God's unwavering presence and of the ultimate fulfillment of our calling through the grace of God.

5. GOD AND THE ATTRACTIVENESS OF OTHER PATHS

Idolatry is a central theme of the prophets and a vital issue of faith in every age. Idolatry is allowing anything other than the love of God to become the primary value shaping one's life. Idols take many forms. They can be any finite, limited thing or any creature which one thinks will be able to satisfy one's greatest needs, and to which religious devotion is given. There are short-term idols and long-term idols, just as there are short-term and long-term needs. Some of the needs that tempt people to idolatry are the need for survival and security in the world, for health and prosperity, for community, for control of our destiny, for freedom from pain, for acceptance and affirmation, or for a lasting sense of personal importance. The problem is not in satisfying human needs with creaturely things, for many human needs can only be satisfied in that way. In themselves the creatures that satisfy human needs are gifts of God, according to biblical faith. The problem is in expecting too much of creaturely things and investing too much of ourselves in them. It is also in making the satisfaction of our needs the test of God. If worshiping God fails to satisfy us in the way we expect, it is tempting to try another god.

Alternative gods, and the paths of living that go with them, become attractive when one's world collapses and the alternate paths seem to be working for other people. Following the popular gods works at least some of the time. That is what makes it so difficult to persuade people to give them up. The prophets warn that other gods will let people down in the long run but urgent needs take precedence in people's minds over prophetic ideals.

Many prophetic texts deal with idolatry. In Isaiah 2:6-22, the third pericope in the prophetic canon warns that in the day of wrath the idols will be thrown away, for in the great crises of life idols let you down. Jeremiah 2 expresses incomprehension over the folly of abandoning the God of the ages for gods close at hand. Idolatry is the pervasive theme of the book of Hosea, as it is of much of Jeremiah 1–25 and Ezekiel 1–24. These are the most obvious texts, but there are many others. All together they form a litany of protest over human lust for power, wealth, and sensual gratification in the pursuit of other gods and at the expense of justice, compassion, and peace (*shalom*), in obedience to the God of the covenant.

We have chosen Jeremiah 44 as our text on this theme. The reasons for the choice are that it makes clear, more than most prophetic texts on the subject, why idolatry is so attractive, and it deals with forms of idolatry that are still tempting people today. The first such form is the belief that worshiping God will produce material benefits for the worshiper. The second is the tendency to think of the living God as a male god. And the third is the tendency to worship a female god.

The way Jeremiah speaks in the narrative seems to suggest elements of both the first and second of these notions; therefore, we must be careful about how we use this text. If God does not provide special material rewards to people for worshiping God, then God does not do this for anyone, regardless of the way he or she speaks about God. Calling God "the Lord" is no more effective in this regard than calling God "the Queen of Heaven." We cannot wrest extra material benefits from God by our worship, whatever its form. Secondly, we cannot represent God truly by pitting a male god against a female god, since both are idols. The living God is beyond gender.

The structure of the sermon. The sermon has a two-part structure. Part one is an *exposition* of the biblical narrative about the dispute between Jeremiah and the Judean refugees (*Looking for a God Who Satisfies Our Needs*). It centers on the theological question at the heart of their dispute. This part of the sermon defines the problem and suggests the resolution of the problem. Part two affirms the new possibility for us and is an exposition of the parallel situation in the church today. It is informed by the message of the text but goes beyond it (*A Faith without Idols*). This part includes a call for repentance and renewal of understanding of who God is.

THE LIVING GOD OR THE KING OR QUEEN OF HEAVEN? A SERMON ON JEREMIAH 44

Then all the men . . . and all the women . . . a great assembly . . . answered Jeremiah, "As for the word that you have spoken to us in the name of the Lord, we are not going to listen to you. Instead, we will do everything that we have vowed. . . . We used to have plenty of food, and prospered, and saw no misfortune. But from the time we stopped making offerings to the queen of heaven and pouring out libations to her, we have lacked everything and have perished by the sword and by famine." (Jeremiah 44:15-18)

Jeremiah preaches a bitter sermon to the men and women who are fleeing from the Babylonian destruction of the land of Judah for safety in Egypt, the perennial place of refuge from famine and war. Jeremiah insists upon interpreting the devastation of Judah in the light of God's wrath. The nation has been punished for its idolatry and refusal to heed the prophets. The people are in exile because of God's profound anger. But the primary problem for Jeremiah is not the people's past action; it is their present behavior. They are continuing to provoke God by their idolatrous worship. Yet, in spite of Jeremiah's preaching of judgment and further calamity, the people refuse to listen. Loudly, they vow to redouble their efforts. Why were the Judeans so resolute in their worship, and who were they worshiping?

Looking for a God Who Satisfies Our Needs [The Problem]

The Queen of Heaven, in her various forms, was the most popular deity in the ancient world. She was depicted as the great mother goddess who was also by turns the virgin warrior and lover. She was known as Ishtar in Mesopotamia, as Asherah in

Canaan, and as Isis in Egypt, among other guises. She was loved and worshiped because she seemed to satisfy the innermost needs of people. She seemed closer to them than the fierce male gods of state and more relevant to their ordinary lives. Worship of her violated the covenant with the God of Israel, but it persisted in Israel just the same.

The Judeans in our story were abandoning the God of Israel for the Queen of Heaven, because they were convinced that if they had been faithful to the Queen of Heaven they would not have been forced into exile. And now that they were in exile, they thought their best chance of flourishing again was to worship her once more. Israel's God had let them down terribly. Although they worshiped God, their world collapsed around them, so they would have no more of God.

Jeremiah had another interpretation of the situation. He did not deny that the calamity had befallen the Judeans. The kingdom had been completely destroyed, and they had been driven from their homes. But Jeremiah viewed the calamity as God's punishment for the people's idolatry. Both the prophet and the people held God responsible for the calamity, but the prophet interpreted it as God's just punishment for idolatry, while the people interpreted it as proof of God's weakness.

The Judeans may have had other reasons as well for abandoning God. The men in the story considered their wives to be the instigators of worship of the Queen of Heaven (44:15), and the female metaphors naming this god must have had a special appeal for them. Women had little role in the worship of Israel's God, and the lure of a female god must have been powerful. We have only to read the famous account of Isaiah's call to prophecy, in Isaiah 6, to realize how common it was to portray Israel's God as the king of heaven, a powerful male image. Yet, whatever appeal the gender of the Queen of Heaven may have had for the women, the men of Judah seem to have followed their wives in worshiping her because worshiping Israel's God had not produced the results they expected. They had not received the material benefits they wanted and believed they deserved.

Jeremiah could do nothing to stop the Judeans from worshiping as they chose to do. In the end he realized that their minds were made up, and he told them to go ahead and fulfill their vows to the Queen of Heaven and, of course, to accept the consequences.

He reminded the people of the fruits of idolatry. They would suffer and die in Egypt—through warfare, famine, and disease. No one would survive the hardships of exile. Furthermore, they would sacrifice their vocation under God to be a light to the nations. Instead of blessing those who encountered them, they would become a mockery and a curse. They would cut themselves off from God's presence in the inner life of the community, and no longer would anyone speak of the living God, the creator of heaven and earth. The narrative ends at this awful impasse between the prophet and the people.

Faith Without Idols [The Possibility for Us]

What do Jeremiah's words mean for us today? Certainly, we must choose between faith in God and faith in idols. Self-interest bordering on idolatry infects everyone's religion. And the judgment of God upon our failure to love and serve God fully is real. It manifests itself in countless ways in the relations of persons and communities. God "withdraws" from people as they withdraw from God. Love diminishes, justice languishes, and the radiance of grace is lost.

Like Jeremiah we can discern God's judgment working in human history, especially in the consequences of our sinful behavior. And yet we cannot simply accept Jeremiah's view of the way God's judgment works. We cannot believe as he seemed to do that God determines the events of history and manipulates natural processes in response to human virtue. We cannot believe that God punishes idolatry by famine and disease. Our experience leads us to conclude that calamity and suffering are a natural part of life and are often beyond human control or influence. Many of the great calamities of nature and history are not caused by people's failure to love God and their neighbors, though these calamities are surely occasions for people to reexamine their lives and to make a deeper commitment to love God and their neighbors.

What is particularly significant for us today is the struggle between a female god and a male god that is implied by this passage. The fact that the Judeans were worshiping the Queen of Heaven, a female deity, implies that they regarded the God of Israel as a male deity, as "the King of Heaven." No doubt this was the common understanding in Israel, for the metaphor of God as king continues to be used even in our own language about God. Jeremiah said nothing to challenge the notion of God as king. But we must avoid the pitfall of taking this metaphor literally. God is not male, any more than God is female. Nor is God *both* male and female. The living God has no gender. Only creatures have gender. To ascribe gender to God is to create an idol in our minds. Let there be no mistake about this: female metaphors are as legitimate to use for God as male metaphors, so long as we are clear that they are metaphors. If we use male metaphors exclusively, they imply that God may in fact be male. So let us avoid using only male metaphors of God, lest we use them idolatrously.

The most fundamental issue of faith is actually deeper than the question of what kinds of metaphors we use to name God. It is the reality of God that is most important in the dispute between the prophet Jeremiah and the Judean people. There is only one God who is the creator, sustainer, and redeemer of life. There is only one God who calls the covenant people into being and demands their obedience to the terms of the covenant. The living God can be called father or mother, King or Queen of Heaven. Many metaphors can be used if they communicate effectively and are recognized for what they are, rich images that help men and women to know and speak about God. It is the reality of God that is ultimately at stake, and not merely the names of God.

The Bible, which was written by men, gives us little insight into the perspectives and special needs of women in ancient Israel. Therefore, we can only speculate about these. In the narrative of Jeremiah 44 the women are said to worship the Queen of Heaven because Yahweh, the Lord of Israel, failed to bless them materially as they wanted him to. Was there more to it than this? Did the Queen of Heaven appeal to them more than Yahweh did because of her gender? We cannot know about those ancient, silent women, but we certainly know of the frustration and pain that women of more recent times, whose voices have found expression, have experienced in the religious community. Only now are women beginning to be treated in the church in the way they deserve, as equal partners with men in every aspect of the church's life, including its leadership. And only now are we beginning to acknowledge the negative consequences, for women and men, of rigid adherence to traditional masculine language for God.

It is time for repentance, and for a new openness to the leading of God's Spirit in our life as the people of God. Men and women must repent in different ways, of course, because they do not share equal responsibility for what has been. But we must share equally in responding to the call of God to find new ways of expressing our faith in the one true God, and new ways of embodying our love of God in deeds of love and justice among all God's beloved creatures.

6. FAITH IN GOD IN TIMES OF PERPLEXITY

Many prophetic texts deal with the certainties of the life of faith: covenant-making, community-formation and -reformation, God's judging and saving acts in history. However, some texts deal with the great uncertainties. Is there any word from God in times of great historical and social upheaval? When chaos reigns, what can the prophet say? The exile was the time of utmost calamity during the prophetic era, and the prophets who spoke most directly to the experience of uncertainty were Jeremiah and Habakkuk. Jeremiah's response is discussed in the next section of this chapter. Now we want to suggest how the preacher can develop a sermon on Habakkuk's message.

Habakkuk deals with a difficult question: How can we have faith in the righteousness of God when injustice and suffering prevail in our lives and in our world? We are using the famous quotation from Habakkuk 2 as our sermon text. However, before attempting to preach on this passage, study the entire book of Habakkuk in order to see how the passage fits into Habakkuk's overall message. Habakkuk was a contemporary of Jeremiah and Ezekiel, and he perceived the perplexities of history as acutely as these other, better-known prophets. His response in the light of faith is as eloquent and as memorable as theirs.

The structure of the sermon. The sermon has a problem-reso-lution-new possibility structure, which follows closely the de-velopment of the ideas in the book of Habakkuk. The sermon is thus essentially expository of the biblical text, and the contem-porary application is integral to the exposition itself. The prob-lem is the incongruity between faith in a just God and the evident injustice of history (*Longing for Justice*). The resolution is the renewal of faith as a personal commitment to God even in the midst of injustice (*Faith in the Face of Injustice*). The new possibility is affirmation of trust in the ultimate triumph of God's justice and joy in the life of faithful obedience (*Rejoicing in Spite of Deprivation*).

WAITING IN FAITH WHILE THE VISION TARRIES: A SERMON ON HABAKKUK 2

O Lord, how long shall I cry for help, and you will not listen? Or cry to you, "Violence!" and you will not save? Why do you make me see wrong-doing and look at trouble? Destruction and vio-lence are before me; strife and contention arise. So the law becomes slack and justice never prevails. The wicked surround the righteous—therefore justice comes forth perverted. . . . Write the vision; make it plain on tablets, so that a runner may read it. For there is still a vision for the appointed time; it speaks of the end and does not lie. If it seems to tarry, wait for it; it will surely come, it will not delay. Look at the proud! Their spirit is not right in them, but the righteous live by their faith. (Hab. 1:2–2:3)

Longing for Justice [The Problem]

The prophet Habakkuk lived during a time of political tur-moil and human suffering. The kingdom of Judah, the last remnant of the glorious kingdom of David and Solomon, had been crushed by the great powers of the Middle East, and life as the people of the covenant had known it had come to an end. The kingship was abolished, their homes and sanctuaries were destroyed, their cities were burned, their leaders were deported, and their land and a few survivors were left desolate. The sacred story of God and Israel seemed tragically at an end.

For Habakkuk, the fall of Israel was not itself a theological stumbling block because he believed that God would punish a sinful nation, even if it were Israel; therefore, like the rest of the prophets, he read God's judgment in the tragic events of Israel's history. The theological problem arose for Habakkuk when he surveyed the whole world scene and realized that tyrannical and godless nations were conquering the people of God, who were surely no more sinful than they. How could the victories of such nations—Assyria, Egypt, Babylonia—possibly reflect the justice of God? Habakkuk's question is blunt, "O Lord, my God . . . your eyes are too pure to behold evil, and you cannot look on wrongdoing; why do you look on the treacherous, and are silent when the wicked swallow those more righteous than they?" (Hab. 1:12-13). We should have no trouble understanding Habakkuk's perplexity, for events in the twentieth-century, especially the Holocaust and other monstrous deeds of genocide, have amply confirmed the prophet's observation that the wicked devour the righteous.

This was the really hard question: Why does a righteous God allow unjust people to violate and destroy the lives of those who are powerless? Habakkuk put this question to God, but he found no immediate answer. Nevertheless, his questioning deepened and clarified his faith. And it was then that he expressed the conviction stated in our text: Though the vision tarries, wait for it, it will surely come at the appointed time. Though cruelty and injustice prevail on all sides, God's justice will eventually be realized among all nations and peoples.

Faith in the Face of Injustice [The Resolution]

The prophet directs his agonizing question to God and then searches for the meaning of undeserved suffering. In his imagination he climbs to the top of a watch tower and looks out through the darkening night, searching for a vision that will make sense of Israel's life among the ruins of the past. And the answer that comes to him is that the righteous will live by their faith. What does faith mean for the prophet? Faith is our trusting response to God's gracious presence in our lives. It comes from the depths of one's being and shapes one's whole relation to the world and one's whole attitude toward life. Habakkuk contrasted those who live by faith with those who are proud and arrogant, who lack spiritual strength and must devour others in their anxious search for satisfaction and security. But living by faith also stands in contrast to despairing and self-loathing, which also destroy the soul but from within. Faith in God does not hold us tightly bound within ourselves but opens us up to face the whole of life and the future, no matter what they may hold for us.

When Habakkuk says the righteous will live by faith even in a world filled with injustice, he is not saying that the righteous will merely *hope* for a better world in the future. Rather he is saying that righteous people will *live* righteously, right now in the present, and it is understood that that will be their contribution to the working out of God's purpose in the course of human events. The righteous will not only wait patiently in hope, they will live and act faithfully, as God's eyes and hands and feet, in the midst of an unrighteous world.

Most of the prophets had a great deal to say about the responsibilities that accompany the journey of faith, but that was not Habakkuk's point. He was asking about the meaning of faith itself during times of perplexity and helplessness, when responsible human action seems futile. As a prophet of God, Habakkuk's vocation was to interpret the acts and demands of God for the covenant community. But he found himself confronting massive injustice in the world, which he and the rest of Israel were powerless to change, and he realized that he could no longer see the hand of the righteous God at work in history. Therefore, as a prophet, all he could do was to wait patiently for his cloudy vision to become clear. He learned that there are limits to what human beings can do in the circumstances of history, as well as limits of human perception into the ways of God.

Why is God so silent when the innocent suffer at the hands of those who betray and destroy? God's answer to Habakkuk was a deepening awareness of God's presence, in his own life and in the lives of those who suffer. Habakkuk reminded himself and the community of faith that in such times, "the righteous live by their faith," or in somewhat different words, "the righteous live in faithfulness." When our choices are few and our time limited, we can still entrust our final destiny to the loving hands of God; and when we do that, we claim our human dignity even in the midst of unjust suffering, knowing that God suffers with us, and that God will complete the meaning of our broken lives in God's own way.

That is the message Habakkuk was commanded to proclaim to the community of faith. Write the vision down and wait for it to come to pass. His command was to paint the vision on a billboard so everyone could see and share it, even as they walked the darkened path before them in the troubled circumstances of their times.

Rejoicing in Spite of Deprivation [The New Possibility]

Habakkuk, then, encouraged the covenant community to live in hope for the ultimate triumph of God's justice, and, meanwhile, to live faithfully in the present moment. But he did one thing more: he promised to rejoice.

> Though the fig tree does not blossom, and no fruit is on the vines;
> though the produce of the olive fails, and the fields yield no food;
> though the flock is cut off from the fold, and there is no herd in the stalls,
> yet I will rejoice in the Lord; I will exult in the God of my salvation.
> God, the Lord, is my strength;
> (God) makes my feet like the feet of a deer,
> and makes me tread upon the heights. (3:17-19)

When Habakkuk, the watchful survivor, declared, from the depths of his perplexity over the ruin of a way of life and the death of an entire population, that he would rejoice in God, he promised something very difficult. It is not easy to rejoice in such times, and we should not speak as if it were easy. Some people are never able to rejoice. Broken by abuse or atrocity, they may perish outright or lose the will to live. It is best to say as little as possible to those who suffer. One should simply offer oneself and one's love to them.

There is wisdom in the story of the visit of Job's three friends to comfort him in his great suffering. They traveled some distance to be with their friend, and when they first saw him, diseased, destitute, and bereaved by the death of his children, "they sat with him on the ground for seven days and seven nights, and no one spoke a word to him, for they saw that his suffering was very great" (Job 2:13). Eventually the three friends forgot themselves and tormented Job with a torrent of words, but for the first seven days they proved themselves wise and compassionate by simply staying there with him. In the end Job learned to rejoice even in the midst of his deprivation, not because of his friends' easy answers to his questions about the justice of God, but as a result of his own prolonged spiritual struggle.

How does one come to rejoice as Habakkuk did? This is one of the profound mysteries of the journey of faith. In Habakukk's case, we know that his perplexity turned into a deeper awareness of God's claim upon his life and a deeper awareness of God's presence. His awareness welled up in rejoicing. It may be that we, too, will come to rejoice in God through a long struggle over the meaning of our life and the events of our time.

Like Habakkuk we seek a vision of the triumph of God's grace in the lives of suffering people, not as a substitute for our acts of love and justice but as a stimulus and guide. Injustice and suffering may frustrate our vision, but in the midst of them we may acquire deeper wisdom. And we too may know the joy of loving God even when the harvest fails. Habakkuk learned, in the midst of Israel's shattered life, that there can be a new vision for those who trust in God and who live their lives in a way that honors those who never had the chance to rejoice in God.

7. God's Providential Care

We are seldom concerned about God's providence when our lives are happy and successful. But when tragedy occurs, we ask about God's providence. Where is God? What is God doing?

The prophets of Israel seemed to be able to discern God's guiding presence in their lives and the life of the covenant community. The prophets may sometimes give the impression that God is in control of every event of life, but this impression is misleading. Fuller reflection on the prophetic witness makes it clear that they considered people to be creative shapers of events. God neither "foresees" nor determines the events of human history apart from human action. Our creaturely freedom is limited but genuine and we are fully responsible before God for our actions. The future is truly open, for us and for God. God is present with us, judging, forgiving, and recreating a righteous people, who are called to serve God faithfully wherever they are.

God's providential care is manifest to eyes of faith within the events of our lives, sustaining and guiding us. Although we may not understand immediately the meaning of cataclysmic events in our personal lives or in our world, we can trust that all things ultimately will find their place in God's judging and forgiving love.

We have selected Jeremiah 29:1-14 as the text for a sermon on the theme of God's providence. It contains a letter of Jeremiah to the Jewish exiles in Babylon, written sometime between the first Judean deportation (598 B.C.E.) and the final destruction of Jerusalem (587 B.C.E.). The exiles were hoping for a speedy return to Judah and for restoration of their life as it had been. Some prophets among them were supporting this hope, even assuring them that God would restore them within two years. Jeremiah interpreted the will of God for the community quite differently. He counseled the exiles to settle down for a long life in Babylonia. And he assured the exiles that their relationship with God was as real in Babylon as in Judah and that they should not isolate themselves spiritually from the Babylonian people, but take an interest in them and make their new environment their home. God's guiding presence would be fully evident to them there, if they sought God with all their hearts.

The structure of the sermon. The sermon has a two-part structure. The first part tells the story of Jeremiah's communication with the Jewish exiles (*Land of Abandonment or Land of Opportunity?*). The text describes the problem facing the exiles, the resolution of the problem proposed by Jeremiah, and the new possibility opened up for the exiles. The second part of the sermon deals with the relevance of Jeremiah's message for us today (*Every Land Is a Holy Land*).

THE PROVIDENCE OF GOD IN THE WAKE OF CALAMITY: A SERMON ON JEREMIAH 29

Thus says the Lord of hosts, the God of Israel, to all the exiles whom I have sent into exile from Jerusalem to Babylon: Build houses and live in them, plant gardens and eat what they produce. Take wives and have sons and daughters. . . . Seek the welfare of the city where I have sent you into exile, and pray to the Lord on its behalf, for in its welfare you will find your welfare. (Jeremiah 29:4-7)

Land of Abandonment or Land of Opportunity?

The calamities of history take on different meanings for different people. Even prophets of God find different significance in the same event. This does not mean that prophets are unreliable but that each personal experience of calamity is distinctive. So too is the way we understand and respond to what has been written. Indeed, while prophets may illuminate the events of our lives, we must take personal responsibility for the way that we live them.

The Babylonian exile was the greatest calamity in the life of ancient Israel. Yet two great prophets of the time, Jeremiah and Ezekiel, responded quite differently to it as counselors of the religious community. Both interpreted the fall of the nation as a judgment of God, and after the fall both encouraged the exiles to trust in God's grace; but they interpreted the exile itself differently. They expressed two classic religious responses to the experience of social cataclysm. Ezekiel viewed Babylonia as a land of wrath, where the exiles would suffer abandonment by God as a punishment of the sinful kingdom of Judah, while Jeremiah viewed Babylonia as a place of interaction with God, as a "land of opportunity." This is the message of Jeremiah's letter to the exiles in chapter 29. The letter is unique in the prophetic literature, but its message is relevant for many a troubled time.

Jeremiah gave the Jewish exiles some very practical advice, not in the sense that it provided a solution to the practical problems of day-to-day living but in the sense that it suggested an attitude and a motive for coping with a new environment and finding fulfillment in it. For this reason Jeremiah's letter is a model of pastoral advice. It helped a defeated people to renew their faith in God and respond constructively to life in an alien world.

The writer of the 137th psalm, who was a contemporary of Jeremiah's, uttered the sentiment of exiled Jews in the familiar words, "How could we sing the Lord's song in a foreign land" (Ps. 137:4). The psalmist lamented the loss of the beloved "land of God," where it was right and proper to sing the Lord's song, and ended the lament with a vengeful cry against the despoilers of the Judean people, "O daughter Babylon, you devastator! Happy shall they be who pay you back what you have done to us! Happy shall they be who take your little ones and dash them against the rock!" (Ps. 137:8-9). Who among the surviving remnant of Judah could help having feelings like this? It is an understandable reaction to shattering personal tragedy. It is all the more remarkable, then, that the prophet Jeremiah, who lived through the same destruction of Jerusalem and shared the same tragic loss as the psalmist, expressed no hatred of Babylon in his letter to the Jewish exiles. Instead, he exhorted them to "seek the welfare of the city where [God has] sent you into exile, and pray to the Lord on its behalf, for in its welfare you will find your welfare" (Jer. 29:7).

Surely Jeremiah must have lamented the children who died in the destruction of Judah. However, in his pastoral letter he spoke not about the children who had died in Jerusalem but about the children who would be born in Babylon. Life would go on, and in Jeremiah's view the faithful thing for the exiles to do was to live as normally as possible, not only among themselves but in relation to the Babylonians as well. He went so far as to encourage the exiles to seek the welfare of the city of Babylon and to pray to God, and to trust God, in the life which they were given, in the place where they found themselves. This was the key to their future, to discern God's guiding presence among them wherever they were, as they sought God with all their hearts and all their understanding.

Every Land Is a Holy Land

In a sense every land is a foreign land for the covenant people, though some lands seem more foreign than others. Tension always exists between the values of the covenant and those of the world. How shall the covenant community live in the midst of this tension? The answer is the same no matter what the circumstances are, yet it is different in every case. To live by faith in a gracious God is always the same fundamental requirement wherever the community finds itself, but the material and social ordering of the community's life is bound to be different in each new place and each new time. Furthermore, the specific problems of relating to the larger culture are constantly changing. The best symbol of the house of God is not a cathedral but a movable tent. In times of rapid social change and great social mobility few people can enjoy the luxury of permanence. Governments rise and fall; economies change; vast numbers of people move; nothing remains the same.

Jeremiah's letter to the exiles reflects his capacity to see beyond the short-term wishes of the exiles to their long-term welfare. Their immediate wish was to return to Palestine. However, this was an unrealistic dream in Jeremiah's view. Therefore, he counseled them to refashion their communal life in the place where they found themselves, and to trust in God's guidance in the enterprise. Jeremiah's letter promises an eventual return, but only after three generations. By this time-table the people who read the letter would live out their entire lives and die in Babylon. Therefore, if they were to have any life at all as the people of God, it would have to be in Babylon and nowhere else. Faith in the God of the covenant left them no option except to follow Jeremiah's advice. If they were to maintain their identity in continuity with the experience of the past, they would have to learn how to sing the Lord's song in a foreign land. As it turned out, when the Persians conquered Babylonia sixty years later and gave the exiled Jews permission to return to Jerusalem, only a few of them did so. Those alive at that time had all been born in Babylonia and had lived their whole lives there, and they preferred to remain in their Babylonian homeland. They learned well how to "sing the Lord's song in a foreign land" and to be faithful to the covenant between God and Israel, for they experienced God's guiding presence where they were.

Jeremiah's letter to the exiles contained a radical message for the Judean people, and its witness to the working of God's providence remains a radical word of faith for the covenant people today. First, it affirms that any land can be "the holy land" for the people of God, which includes us, since God's presence and grace are with us everywhere we go. It is necessary for us to open ourselves to the power of God in faith. But it is also necessary to let go of the past, however painful that may be. Jeremiah's advice was not cheap or superficial but realistic and faithful. He knew what it meant to lose everything and to live solely by faith.

Second, Jeremiah's counsel suggests that isolation from the surrounding community is not God's will for the covenant people. Ultimately, the well-being (*shalom*) of God's people is intertwined with that of all people, for all people are equally loved by God, and God calls us to love all those whom God loves. Finally, while it is right for us to trust in the future which God has in store for us, it is futile to insist that the future conform to our own design. Most of us like to plan the future using familiar models from the past. Yet, all old models must eventually give way in the face of new needs and new leadings of the Spirit of God. According to Jeremiah, the unknown future is not to be feared on this account but is to be accepted as a gift of God whatever the circumstances of life may be, in the sure knowledge that God is always present to guide and sustain us.

Chapter Five

Preaching from the Prophets on Contemporary Issues

T he preacher stands between the biblical text and the
modern situation as a representative interpreter for the
people of God. The dialogue between text and situation
which the preacher articulates is always two-way, regardless
of where it begins. In the last chapter we began with the text
and moved toward the contemporary situation. In this chapter we reverse the process, taking the contemporary situation
as the starting point and moving back to the biblical text.
Before, we focused on major themes of the prophetic corpus;
now we focus on a number of crucial issues confronting the
church today. These issues are ethical, but at the same time
they are theological, for in the prophetic witness the two
dimensions of covenantal experience are inseparable. We
cannot know or serve God independently of our moral commitment to other persons, and we cannot fulfill our moral
commitment without knowing God. Our covenant with God
is at the same time a covenant with other persons. Consequently, theological and ethical dimensions are present in
each of the themes we are considering in this chapter.

Since the ethical teaching of the prophets is extensive, the
task of appropriating their teaching into the witness of the
church today might appear to be straightforward. On the contrary, it is fraught with difficulty! The difficulty is due in part to
the sheer distance between us and the ancient prophets in time,
place, and language. This distance affects our effort to interpret

the basic themes of the prophets, but in the case of the specific ethical questions with which the church is involved today, the difficulty is compounded because of the difference between ancient Israelite life and our own. The many differences include science and technology, communication, transportation, social organization, government, education, economic organization, health care, the arts, entertainment, housing, and almost every other aspect of life. The difference is so great it amounts to a gulf between the two ways of life. As a result of this gulf, it is not easy to relate the prophetic proclamation to our contemporary social situation. Some of the prophets' problems are not our problems, and quite a few of our problems were not their problems. In fact, many of the issues of social justice that confront us today are the result of the changes that have occurred in the world since biblical times, so it is often difficult to find any connection between our issues and the prophets' messages.

Having prepared ourselves for the difficult task in applying the prophetic message to the ethical problems of our time, it is surprising to discover that many of the moral issues addressed by the prophets are still lively issues today. And, more importantly, we find that the fundamental ethical principles embodied in the prophetic witness are as relevant for the people of God in our time as they were in the prophets' own. The covenant community is called to bear faithful witness to God's love and righteousness through its life and action in its particular time and place in history.

In this chapter, the initial discussion focuses on the general question of the relevance of the prophetic proclamation to modern ethical issues. Next, we deal concretely with several specific issues in the light of the prophetic witness. In each case a range of prophetic texts are considered that have a bearing on the issue, and then a concise sermon on one of those texts is presented. The issues that are addressed include: (1) exclusiveness in the church, (2) Christians and the natural environment, (3) the church and the neediest, (4) God and religious language, (5) the hierarchy and the laity in the church's ministry, and (6) the new covenant and Judaism.

Beginning with the Contemporary Situation

The minister who preaches on a current ethical or social problem is more likely to turn for help to contemporary books on the subject than to the prophets. We know that the prophets are a basic resource for ethical understanding, but we may be frustrated in our search for a pertinent word on a specific social issue. Therefore, our impulse is often simply to locate a text on the basis of a catchword association and develop a sermon more or less independently of the message of the text. In this way the text becomes a springboard, or perhaps a pretext, for our homiletical reflections rather than an integral part of them. When this happens, the application of the biblical text is unconvincing, and it detracts from the sermon rather than enhancing it, even though it seems to lend an aura of sanctity to it. Is there anything we can do instead?

Surely, the first thing we should do is to identify our specific purpose in addressing the topic, in an attempt to stay clearly focused and not wander vaguely around the topic. Is our intention to take a stand on a controversial issue? Is it to stimulate and quicken the congregation's conscience? Is it to reconcile opposing views within the congregation? Is it to guide the congregation's resolve to take action? Is it to deepen understanding of the biblical foundations of Christian responsibility, or perhaps to correct a misinterpretation of the prophets? Is it to console people beset by a problem they are helpless to solve? Because our homiletical intention will inevitably shape our search for the right text, the better we clarify our intention in advance, the less likely we are to use the text unconvincingly. It is better not to use a biblical text at all than to use it inappropriately, for it will only confuse and contribute to the disuse and ignorance of the prophets that is already widespread in the church today. So, whatever else one learns about preaching from biblical texts on contemporary ethical issues, the most important lesson of all is not to use the text merely as a pretext.

The second lesson relates to the recognition of the difference between modern and ancient civilization. The gulf separating us from the social world of the prophets means that we are not likely to find direct answers in the prophetic corpus to the specific social and ethical questions of our time. Take the issue of substance-addiction, for example. The prophets never speak explicitly about this issue. They criticized specific acts of drunkenness (e.g., Isa. 5:11; 28:7-8; and Hos. 7:5), but they were unaware of the social circumstances and genetic predispositions which cause alcoholism and other forms of addiction, or of the many other addictive substances that ravage people's lives today. Therefore, the prophets' writings do not help us deal directly with this complex problem. Much of the contemporary social problem begins where the prophetic discussion leaves off.

Or consider the present problems in the political order. Currently, in almost every country of the world the structures of government differ radically from those that existed in ancient times, particularly in Israel. And the ethical questions that arise because of new forms of government are beyond the ken of the prophetic writers. So it is in the economic order as well. Money, for example, was only beginning to be used in biblical times, and its form was very simple—metal coinage. The vast, intricate, abstract realm of money that we know today, which affects every aspect of our life, was completely unknown in biblical times. Therefore, the prophetic writers could hardly offer us any direct help on the ethical questions posed by a money economy today. Or consider the ethics of health care. Abortion, euthanasia, access to care, standards of professional training and practice, and the cost of care, are only a few aspects of this vast area of our lives that create new ethical questions. Here again, the prophets have nothing directly to say.

Some of the crucial ethical questions we face today are new in relation to the prophetic writings, not because the phenomena from which they arise are new, but because public awareness and discussion of the phenomena are new. An example is the contemporary question of homosexuality. Does it stem from environmental factors, genetic factors, or both? What should the church's attitude toward homosexual persons be? The prophets offer us no help on this question. Even if we extend our search to include the whole Bible, we find very few texts that have any relevance to the question, and those we find refer only to particular homosexual acts and not to homosexuality as an orientation. But it is precisely this latter issue that perplexes the church today. Other similar examples are not hard to find. In virtually every area of life we must deal with difficult ethical questions on which the prophetic books offer no direct counsel.

Another reason why our questions may receive no answers from the prophets is that our questions are often concerned with the morality of individual persons, whereas the prophets were primarily concerned with the ethical responsibility of the covenant community. Individual morality concerned them to the extent that it was representative of the community's morality. For this and other reasons, the counsel we should expect to find in the prophetic books on the concrete ethical issues of our time is likely to be indirect.

If our conclusion is correct—that we should not expect to find prophetic texts dealing directly with the specific ethical issues engaging Christians today, but that we can expect to find texts that are indirectly relevant—then the procedural question is *how* to develop sermons on prophetic texts in such cases. We can state the general *theological* principle that informs our effort to relate the prophetic witness to our contemporary ethical situation, which is that covenantal faithfulness should be manifested in acts of love and justice in our own time and place. However, it is harder to define a *methodological* principle to guide us in the practical task of linking particular ethical issues and particular prophetic texts. The most satisfactory way to answer this practical question, we think, is not to generalize about it, but to discuss specific cases.

Preaching on Contemporary Issues

We have chosen six crucial issues that confront Christians today, as well as the wider human community. Each issue engages the church in many ways, not merely in relation to the task of preaching. But the task undertaken here is to identify texts in the prophetic books that are relevant to these issues and to consider possible ways of utilizing these texts in sermons. Under each topic we first mention various texts that seem to bear on the issue in question, and then we offer a concise sermon on a particular text.

The list of issues chosen is obviously selective; there are other issues that churches are, or should be, addressing today to which the prophetic message can be applied. One such issue is the use of power in communal relations. Another is the relation of ritual worship and social responsibility. A third is the relationship between ownership and stewardship, particularly of land. The list could go on. Our intention here is not to cover the whole range of social issues. Far from it! Our aim instead is merely to illustrate how to use the prophetic text in relation to a specific issue.

1. EXCLUSIVENESS IN THE CHURCH

The church proclaims God's equal love for all God's people, and yet local churches are among the most racially segregated communities in America today. We have tolerated this segregation in recent years in order to affirm the identity and heritage of African-American, Hispanic, and Asian churches, but it is not at all clear that justice and equality have been promoted as a result. It is arguable that there is more exclusiveness in the church today than ever before. Any sort of exclusiveness in the church is a problem. It is a problem for the outsider who is injured or demeaned. It is a problem for the insider who is denied interaction with the rich diversity of God's people. And it is a problem for God, who created the church to bear witness by word and deed to the oneness of humankind.

Today we are more aware of the pain caused by exclusion than the prophets were because more voices are being heard by the covenant community. Nevertheless, the prophets dealt with this issue because there was already a good deal of exclusiveness among the ancient Israelites, and the prophets viewed this tendency as a violation of God's call to deal lovingly with the resident alien (the *ger*) and the foreigner (the *nokri*). The book of Jonah addresses this question, as we have seen in chapter 4, but it deals with a different aspect from the one we are considering here. In Jonah, the issue is whether or not the limits of God's love are wide enough to include foreigners in their own communities. Here the issue is whether or not there are limits on God's love within the covenant community.

The prophetic text which touches most directly and helpfully upon the question of exclusivism in the covenant community is Isaiah 56:1-8, and it is this text which we have picked for our illustrative sermon. The text takes up the specific question of the admission of eunuchs and foreigners to the temple rituals. However, the principle of inclusiveness stated by the writer can be applied to other sorts of persons as well: all those who "love the name of the Lord . . . keep the sabbath . . . and hold fast to (the) covenant" (56:6), should be allowed to participate in communal worship.

Isaiah 56 was written at the time of the second temple of Jerusalem (515 B.C.E.–70 C.E.) and reflects the debate in the cultic community over the question of who should be allowed to participate in Temple worship. At that time eunuchs were excluded on the grounds that they were blemished, and foreigners were excluded on the grounds of their ethnic impurity. The exclusion of foreigners was carried to such an extreme that Judean men married to foreign women were required to divorce their wives (Ezra 10), even though divorce meant destitution for many women in the ancient world. Women were also denied full participation in worship and were excluded from the priesthood entirely on the grounds of their sexual impurity, although this particular exclusion is not mentioned in Isaiah 56.

The sermon alludes to some contemporary reasons for discrimination in the church. Discrimination because of race, sex, and physical impairment is clearly parallel to the situation suggested in the text. However, there are other reasons for discrimination today, including social class, poverty, and sexual orientation. The question regarding the full inclusion of gay and lesbian persons in the covenant community differs, for example, from the question regarding women and persons of other races, because sex and race are clearly physical characteristics and not environmental in origin, and there may be an environmental factor in homosexuality.

Every preacher must treat the subject of strangers in God's household in a way that fits his or her own setting. Some congregations consist largely of people who benefit from the social, economic, and racial boundaries that exist in our society, while other congregations are made up of people who are denied full participation in these benefits or are oppressed in other ways by the existence of social boundaries. Still other congregations are mixed in this respect. The particular blend of prophetic criticism and assurance of grace that one adopts in a sermon must depend on the social setting in which the sermon is preached.

The structure of the sermon. The following sermon is composed of three parts. Part one states the problem, in both its ancient and contemporary manifestations (*Exclusiveness in God's House*). Part two affirms the prophetic understanding of God's love which is the basis of its resolution (*God and the Outsider*). And part three spells out the implications of the prophetic affirmation for the community of faith today—the new possibility (*Strangers in the Church*).

GOD AND THE OUTSIDER: A SERMON ON ISAIAH 56

Do not let the foreigner joined to the Lord say, "The Lord will surely separate me from his people"; and do not let the eunuch say, "I am just a dry tree." For thus says the Lord: To the eunuchs who keep my sabbaths . . . and hold fast my covenant, I will give, in my house and within my walls, a monument and a name better than sons and daughters; I will give them an everlasting name that shall not be cut off. And the foreigners who join themselves to the Lord, to minister to him, to love the name of the Lord . . . I will bring to my holy mountain, and make them joyful in my house of prayer . . . for my house shall be called a house of prayer for all peoples. (Isaiah 56:3-7)

Exclusiveness in God's House [The Problem]

"God's house shall be called a house of prayer for all peoples." These are eloquent words, which surely express the goal of the prophetic proclamation of God's grace. Unfortunately, they do not describe the actual practice of the covenant community, either in the prophet's time or in our own. Instead, they represent the voice of the community's conscience, the prophetic voice, calling the community to reaffirm the foundations of its faith and to reform its life accordingly.

The prophet's congregation discriminated against a great many people, including foreigners, women, and the physically impaired. None of these people shared fully in the ritual fellowship or the life of the community. The house of God was not truly a house of prayer for all people but only for "unblemished" males.

The situation in the church is not altogether different today. Ethnic and racial discrimination infects religious congregations as much as it does society at large, women are still subordinate to men in the church's leadership, even in denominations that ordain women, and homosexual persons continue to be unwelcome in most congregations. The worship of God is among the most divisive activities in American life. We have not come far from the ancient Temple!

Why do we exclude people? We set boundaries as marks of our identity as a group. We wear uniforms, perform initiation rites, create symbols, and a common language in order to distinguish ourselves. We do it in baseball teams and military groups, fraternal organizations and social clubs, and in groups of clergy. Religious boundaries, like these other boundaries, begin with good intentions. They identify a group as the people of God, and they define the special commitment one must make to be a part of the group.

The trouble with boundaries is that we forget they are our own creations, and we sanctify them. We confuse our identity and sense of worth with them and then defend them as we defend ourselves. Our boundaries, while ostensibly preserving the sanctity and integrity of God's community, often protect our personal interests and our sense of self. Thus, if we are male, we may feel threatened by sharing our place fully with females, and if we are white, we may feel threatened by sharing it fully with people of color. And so it is with social class, economic status, and sexuality. Thus we exclude people; we set boundaries to God's love.

God and the Outsider [The Resolution]

In the witness of the Bible, God often works through outsiders to shatter Israel's exclusiveness and restore the community to the terms of the covenant. There was Ruth the Moabite, who demonstrated the meaning of loyalty and steadfast love to birthright members of the covenant community. There was Ebed-melech, the Ethiopian eunuch, who saved Jeremiah's life and preserved a great prophetic legacy for the future (Jer. 38:7-13). Cyrus of Persia was a foreign king whom a prophet of Israel called *messiah* for his role in the salvation of the covenant community (Isa. 45:1). And there were many, many more. God is the God of those outside the community as well as those inside, and God works through strangers to bring judgment to the community of faith and call it to repentance. The voice of the prophet continually reminds us that it is God who sets the boundaries of the covenant, not we.

In covenantal faith there are no outsiders. Everyone stands equally before God as God's beloved creature but also as a sinner who has rejected God's love. Being a member of the covenant community does not change our capacity to resist God's love or take away the temptation to sin. The members of the community differ from others only in knowing that it is God whom we turn against when we pursue loveless and selfish ways. Every human being is the object of God's continuous, redeeming love, whether that person is a member of the community of faith or outside it. To "join oneself to God," as our text puts it, requires only trusting faith and loving commitment to God and to all those whom God loves. These are the only requirements stated by the prophet, to love God's name and keep God's covenant. There are no other boundaries. Although we work continually to reset the boundaries according to our own plan, the loving God works to remove our boundaries again and again.

Strangers in the Church [The New Possibility]

The prophetic message of the gift and claim of God's love for all people puts our boundary-building in a searching new light. If we trust God's love for us, we should be able to leave the whole question of physical and social boundaries to God. What is our situation in the covenant community today? How have we responded to the call of God? In the light of the prophetic witness we are forced to admit that most of us are content with the boundaries that exist in the church and have no wish to change them. Most of us feel comfortable in homogeneous congregations and make no effort to include people who are unlike us. Who are the people we exclude because of their race and ethnic background? Who are the people we exclude because of their physical disabilities or sexual characteristics? The prophet's word is a sharp reminder that those we exclude simply on these grounds are loved by God and remembered by God and that they should be welcome participants in God's house.

The prophet's word does not mean that anything goes! He places a restriction upon the stranger and the eunuch. That restriction is the demand that God's love always places over the lives of the faithful: to love God and hold fast to the covenant. But that is the only restriction the prophet places upon those who wish to take part in the life and worship of the people of God. Hear it again: to love God and hold fast to the covenant! The other restrictions that we impose violate God's love.

God is calling the church to new dimensions of obedience today and will surely sustain it as it responds to this call. Becoming truly the household of God in which there are no outsiders is both a responsibility and a privilege. Welcoming the outsider and empowering those who are disempowered strengthens and enriches the church. Exclusion impoverishes the community in the ways that matter most, and disempowerment abases the powerful, too. The promise of God is that those who hold fast to the covenant will have an everlasting memorial. With that sure promise as the foundation of our trust, we can commit ourselves completely to a community whose boundaries are as wide as God's love.

2. CHRISTIANS AND THE NATURAL ENVIRONMENT

Most people today are aware of our responsiblity to care for the natural environment. Local communities recycle trash in order to reduce pollution and conserve natural resources. International coalitions seek to prevent overcutting in the rain forests, overfishing in the seas, and despoiling of the seashores. People everywhere are concerned about nuclear pollution of land and water and the overheating of the atmosphere. We know that we have the technological capacity to destroy our natural environment and the responsibility to prevent it from happening. Yet, much damage has already been done, and some of the damage is irreversible. Clearly this is one of the urgent social issues of our time.

The record of the church in regard to the environment is a sad one, and it badly needs correcting. The church has thought of salvation as only for human beings, ignoring the rest of creation, and it has interpreted human "dominion" over the rest of creation (Gen. 1:26-28) in a way that encourages exploitation of the earth for human ends. The prophetic understanding of the unity and interdependence of all creation provides a powerful corrective to these unfortunate views.

The destructive effects of human irresponsibility upon the natural environment are much greater today than they were in the prophets' time, because our technological capacity to pollute the environment and consume irreplaceable natural resources is vastly greater than that of any ancient people. Therefore, there are no texts in the prophetic books that indicate the scope of the problem in its modern form. Nevertheless, there are prophetic texts that speak eloquently about the interdependence of human beings and the natural environment, as well as the moral and spiritual dimensions of Israel's relation to nature, and these texts are relevant to our attitudes and behavior today.

Second Isaiah proclaimed a new age of salvation for Israel and the nations that included the transformation of the desert into a gardenland (e.g., 41:18-19 and 49:10). In the abundant new life proclaimed by the prophet, a productive relationship between the human community and the earth was indispensable. The idea of the transformation of the desert into a gardenland is also presented vividly in Ezekiel's picture of the coming age. He describes a stream of pure water rising from the temple of God, flowing down from the temple mount into the desert of Judah and the Dead Sea, bringing the desert to verdant life, and turning the salt water sweet (Ezek. 47:1-12). The best known prophetic reference to the transformation of humanity and nature is Isaiah's description of the peaceable kingdom, in Isaiah 11. When leaders govern in the spirit of God, and righteousness reigns among the people, then harmony also prevails in the people's relation to nature (vv. 6-9).

Another pertinent text is Amos 7:1-9, which recounts Amos' visions of God's judgment of Israel. They depict the judgment as the devastation of the natural world. In the first vision, Amos sees the crops upon which the Israelites were dependent for survival being eaten up by locusts (7:1). In the second, he sees a tremendous conflagration vaporizing the sea and consuming the land (7:4). And in the third, he sees God standing beside a crooked wall, the symbol of the unrighteous people, with a plumbline in hand (7:7-8). The wall is not true, so it must be taken down. The cause of God's judgment is Israel's unrighteousness. The manifestation of God's judgment is first of all political and social, as the final threat in Amos's series of visions makes clear (7:9), but it is also the ruination of nature, as the first two threats suggest. Amos understood the powerful link between the human community and the natural environment, both in blessing and in calamity.

The text we have chosen for our sermon is Hosea 2:16-25. It speaks about the covenant that God will establish between Israel and the earth as a part of the renewal of God's own relationship with Israel. Through this covenant, the spoilage of the earth that has marked the present era of Israel's life will be reversed, and justice will be restored. The spoilage of the earth is mentioned in Hosea 4:1-4, to which we will also refer.

The structure of the sermon. Here again is the three part structure we have used in several other sermons. The first part presents the problem (*"The land mourns, and all who live in it languish"*), the second, the resolution (*"I will make for you a covenant on that day"*), and the third, the new possibility for the covenant community (*Our Covenant with the Earth*).

OUR COVENANT WITH THE EARTH:
A SERMON ON HOSEA 2

I will make for you a covenant on that day with the wild animals, the birds of the air, and the creeping things of the ground; and I will abolish the bow, the sword, and war from the land; and I will make you lie down in safety. And I will take you for my wife forever; I will take you for my wife in righteousness and in justice, in steadfast love, and in mercy. I will take you for my wife in faithfulness; and you shall know the Lord. On that day I will answer, says the Lord, I will answer the heavens and they shall answer the earth; and the earth shall answer the grain, the wine, and the oil, and they shall answer Jezreel; and I will sow him for myself in the land. (Hosea 2:18-22)

"The land mourns, and all who live in it languish" [The Problem]

The prophet Hosea believed there was an intimate bond between people and their natural environment, and that people's behavior affected the earth as well as the people themselves. This bond between humanity and the earth was based upon their common dependence upon God, who fashioned and sustained the two together as interdependent parts of a single, unified creation. When the people were faithful in their covenantal responsibility to God, they were also faithful in their stewardship of the earth, and the earth flourished as a result. But when the people's bond with God was broken by their infidelity and unrighteousness, their bond with nature was also distorted, and nature languished.

Hosea perceived the ruination of Israel and the ruination of the land around them, and he viewed the ruination of the land as the consequence of Israel's broken covenant with God. In his view, injustice and infidelity to God affected not only Israel's social environment but also its natural environment. Hear Hosea's charge:

The Lord has an indictment against the inhabitants of the land. There is no faithfulness or loyalty, and no knowledge of God in the land. Swearing, lying, and murder, and stealing and adultery break out; bloodshed follows bloodshed. Therefore, the land mourns and all who live in it languish; together with the wild animals and the birds of the air, even the fish of the sea are perishing. (Hosea 4:1-3)

According to Hosea, a three-step process of destruction was occurring, and one of the results of the process was the destruction of the earth and all the creatures that inhabit it. The process began with the people's lack of faith and knowledge of God. Knowing God truly meant acknowledging God's sovereignty over Israel's life and the earth in which it was lived. The earth and all its creatures were God's, and the fruits of the earth were a gift of God to sustain Israel. Living responsibly in God's good earth meant recognizing the gift and acknowledging the Giver. Righteous living is rooted in knowledge of God and faith in God.

As the knowledge of God and faith in God diminished in Israel, so did the moral integrity of the community. Human relations were spoiled and all the deadly sins that Hosea noted ate away at the fabric of Israel's life. Hosea's oracles are filled with descriptions of Israel's moral and social ruin, from the kingship to the peasantry. Unrighteousness affected every aspect of the community's life: political leadership, ritual practice, the marketplace, even family relations.

This was the second step in the process of Israel's ruin: lack of faith and the knowledge of God resulted in moral corruption. But this was not the last step in the process of ruin. There was a third step, and it was the ruin of the natural environment. Not only was the land filled with the people's religious infidelity and social unrighteousness, it was spoiled for the other creatures who lived in it. Israel's behavior affected its environment, and in this case the effect was devastating.

"I will make for you a covenant on that day" [The Resolution]

The situation that Hosea described in nature and society was grim, but as a man of faith he did not utterly despair over it. He trusted the creator of Israel and the natural environment to renew them both eventually. The ultimate solution to the ruination of the earth, according to Hosea, would come about as a result of Israel's recognition of the gift of God's love and the claim that love placed over their lives. But that was a hope for the future. Meanwhile, until God's love was finally able to lure the people back to faithfulness, they were to suffer the consequences of their idolatry and injustice. The first consequence was the shattering of human relationships and the corruption of society, but the devastation of nature was another. Hosea understood both consequences to be manifestations of God's judgment. "(God) will lay waste her vines and her fig trees," he declared (2:12). The judgment of God, which would be manifested above all in the political conquest and exile of the nation, was punitive, but it was also disciplinary. It would remove the opportunities for Israel's idolatry and injustice and open the way for a new discernment of the ultimate source and end of life—the knowledge and love of God—and therefore for a renewal of the covenant between God and Israel. But this new covenant with the creator would also be a covenant with the whole of creation: the animals, fish, and birds, the plants, and the earth itself. The way ahead was filled with pain and deprivation for Israel; it was not an easy path to follow. But the goal of the experience was the ultimate renewal of Israel's fidelity and righteousness, and with it the renewal of Israel's life and its relationship with creation.

What effect would God's discipline have upon the people, according to the prophet? If the whole earth languished when the people did not know God, then the whole earth would flourish when the people came to know God in righteousness and justice, in steadfast love and fidelity. When the people were reconciled to God in knowledge and fidelity, this reconciliation would affect not only their human relationships but also their relationship to the natural world. "I will make for you a covenant on that day with the wild animals, the birds of the air, and the creeping things of the ground . . . and you shall know the Lord" (2:18-20). The unity of God's creation—the interdependence of all created things—which can lead to the ruination of nature when the human community is spiritually ruined, can also lead to the renewal of nature when the human community is spiritually renewed. And the keys to both renewals, according to the prophetic witness, are people's knowledge and love of God.

Our Covenant with the Earth [The New Possibility]

What relevance do Hosea's oracles have for us as we face the possible devastation of the earth through human selfishness and greed? Hosea and the other prophets of Israel did not understand as fully as we do the mechanisms that lead to the ruin of nature, but they discerned the ruin itself. Their understanding was based on the conviction that God is sovereign over all things and that all creatures in the world are interdependent. They lacked some of the empirical evidence for this interdependence that we have today, but they recognized the fundamental unity of the creation, just the same.

We need to learn the wisdom of the prophets concerning our responsibility for God's creation, for the church lags behind in this. Christians have been more concerned with salvation than with creation, and we have reserved salvation for ourselves—as human beings—and disregarded the rest of creation as unimportant in God's ultimate plan. To make matters worse, we have misused the biblical edict of human dominion over the other creatures, which is part of the creation story in Genesis (Gen. 1:26-28) as a license to exploit the earth's resources selfishly. Now the earth languishes, and it is largely our fault. The prophets knew that the languishing of creation is a sign that people do not know God, and they called the people to repentance.

The message of Hosea for the people of God today is that genuine knowledge and love of God will lead us to do all we can to protect and cherish the natural world, which God created and God loves. The reason for cherishing nature is not only to insure a future for ourselves and for subsequent generations of humankind. To be sure, the future of humanity depends upon our care of the environment today. But, according to the prophetic witness, that is not the only reason to care for nature. The prophets insist that if there is true knowledge of God in the covenant community, there will be harmony and peace between human beings and the rest of creation. All living beings are interrelated parts of one created world, and human beings, who possess the unique power to destroy and to construct, also have unique responsibility for the flourishing of the other creatures. The prophets linked the defilement of nature to idolatry, which resulted from ignorance of God, and the renewal of nature to covenant faithfulness, which resulted from knowledge of God. The ultimate motive for loving and honoring the natural world is not self-interest, but the love of God, who has made all the creatures in the world.

Some things change with time. Today we can wreak havoc upon nature to an extent that was inconceivable in the prophets' time. Other things do not change. We suffer the natural consequences of idolatry and unrighteousness in our time, just as people did in the prophets' time. But if the people of God truly know God, they will live in such a way as to be in harmony with nature. We are interdependent parts of the marvelous world in which we all live out our days—animals, plants, and human beings together—and we, as human beings, must cherish and care for this world. The church cannot solve the vast environmental problems that exist today. That is not the church's responsibility. But the church can repent of its flawed view of humanity's relation to the earth, and can bear witness to God's love for the whole creation. The church can testify to the world that ignoring creation means ignoring God, and that caring for the creation is our sacred duty and privilege.

3. THE CHURCH AND THE NEEDIEST

The destitution of the neediest in our society haunts our conscience, as millions suffer, and efforts to alleviate their misery fall short. The response of the church is mixed. Some churches have soup kitchens and help the homeless, while some churches are preoccupied with their own needs and are content to let others, especially the government, help the neediest. Or they simply ignore poverty. This issue is not new. The same problem existed in ancient Israel. The prophetic books are full of complaints about the callousness and irresponsibility of the religious community. The prophets do not propose concrete ways of eliminating poverty, nor do they promise that the problem will ever be solved. They say nothing about who should bear the responsibility for the poor, the government or the private sector. However, the prophets do have something to say about the neediest in the light of the covenant faith. Above all, they make it clear that this is a *theological* issue for them. God hears the cries of suffering people and participates in their suffering. To fail to share God's compassion for those in need is to fail to understand the meaning of covenant faithfulness and the gift and claim of God's love.

For *Amos*, seeking God means acting justly toward the poor, and oppressing the poor means threatening the very life of the people of God (Amos 5:4-15). *Micah* considers it more important to do justice and show kindness than to maintain ritual worship of God (Mic. 6:6-8), and he locates the theological grounds for doing justice in God's act of redemption of Israel from slavery (Mic. 6:3-4). The answer to the prophet's question of what the Lord requires is to act with the same compassion the Lord has shown to Israel. In *Isaiah's* famous messianic oracle, the one who leads Israel in the Spirit of God acts justly toward the poor and powerless of the earth (Isa. 11:1-4). *Jeremiah* characterizes the idolatrous community as one that exploits the needy (Jer. 5:18-29). Because God cares for the needy, acknowledging who God is leads to the same kind of care. This affirmation lies close to the heart of *Second Isaiah's* message as well. God responds to the plight of the poor and needy (Isa. 41:17-20), and so, too, must the true servant of God (42:1-9). These references could be multiplied many times over in the prophetic books. The theme continues into the New Testament as well. We need only recall the famous passage in Matthew 25:31-46 about inheriting a place in the kingdom of heaven. It is reserved for those who feed the hungry, welcome strangers, clothe the naked, and visit the prisoners!

No passage in the prophetic books states the case more forcefully than Isaiah 58. It raises the fundamental religious question of whether the service of God consists primarily of worship or of works of love for suffering people. In what measure does God require these two types of acts, and how are they related to each other? We may recall the commission of Moses that set in motion God's great act of redemption. Moses was to bring the Israelites to the mountain of God to worship, but he was first of all to free them from slavery in Egypt (Exod. 3:12). The author of Isaiah 58, one of the anonymous contributors to the post-exilic collection of oracles known as Third Isaiah (Isaiah 56–66), obviously stressed works of love over ritual observances, just as Amos did in the famous passage, "I hate, I despise your festivals . . . but let justice roll down" (Amos 5:21-

24). Another way of stating the question with which Isaiah 58 is concerned is to ask whether God is more interested in satisfying the personal needs of the worshiping congregation or in relieving the suffering of the needy. This question has startling relevance to every Christian congregation in the world today!

The structure of the sermon. The sermon has three parts. The first part defines the problem (*Is Our Worship Acceptable to God?*), the second states the prophetic resolution of the problem (*Acts of Worship Are Not Enough!*), and the third suggests the new possibility for us (*Service Acceptable to God*).

The Oppressed and the Homeless: A Sermon on Isaiah 58

"Why do we fast, but you do not see? Why humble ourselves, but you do not notice?" Look, you serve your own interest on your fast day, and oppress all your workers. . . . Is such the fast that I choose, a day to humble oneself? Is it to bow down the head like a bulrush, and to lie in sackcloth and ashes? Will you call this a fast, a day acceptable to the Lord? Is not this the fast that I choose: to loose the bonds of injustice . . . to let the oppressed go free . . . to share your bread with the hungry, and bring the homeless poor into your house; when you see the naked to cover them? . . . Then your light shall break forth like the dawn, and your healing shall spring up quickly. . . . Then you shall call, and the Lord will answer; you shall cry for help, and he will say, Here I am. (Isaiah 58:3-9)

Is Our Worship Acceptable to God? [The Problem]

Why do we have worship services? Why do we sing hymns and read scripture? Why do we pray? Why do we engage in spiritual disciplines like fasting? There are many good reasons why we worship God. We derive great personal benefit from participating in worship and in the spiritual disciplines. Many of us believe that the week goes by more smoothly and that we can handle life's daily tasks much more faithfully when we turn to a regular means of grace. And we certainly come to a greater awareness of God's presence and love through the spiritual disciplines. There is obvious benefit for our families. When children and parents participate in the life of a worshiping fellowship, and in its festive services and programs, that family is stabilized and strengthened. The congregation itself is up-lifted and sustained by worship services. Certainly there is huge benefit for society itself. Doesn't every society benefit by having responsible, God-fearing citizens? Last but not least, all of us at some level or another truly believe that the acts of worship we perform are pleasing to God. Our acts of worship and spiritual discipline are what God wants from us, are they not?

The prophet who wrote Isaiah 58 was part of the congrega-tion in Jerusalem in the fifth-century B.C.E. This congregation had every reason to be satisfied with its worship. Their sanc-turary was enviable in size and furnishings, though it was certainly not ostentatious. Their clergy were a select group of educated men, all of whom were ordained in the proper Leviti-cal tradition. Even the choir was polished and well-rehearsed. The congregation's calendar was filled with weekly and monthly activities and worship services, in addition to the great seasonal festivals. And all of this was supported by faithful and willing tithers. It was every minister's dream come true! Yet, the prophet who proclaimed our text was not content with the way things were.

The occasion for his protest was a time of community fasting, and the prophet's first word was about the people's motives in observing the fast. Fasting is a religious practice hallowed by tradition, and those who fast as a spiritual discipline realize that it heightens their spiritual perception. However, according to the prophet, the people fasted in order to get God's attention, and to extract a special blessing from God. And because the benefit they wanted did not come, they complained to God, "Why humble ourselves, but you do not notice?"

Now someone could ask, "How did the prophet know that the people's motives were self-serving?" Was he being fair? Judging people's motives is a tricky business at best. Did the prophet really know the people's hearts? The reason the prophet thought the people's worship was self-serving was that he knew they were self-serving in other dimensions of their life. They quarreled and fought among themselves, in the home and in the market place. And they oppressed their workers. The prophet considered the people's worship hypocritical because it had no noticeable effect upon their daily lives!

This is a prophetic word that religious people don't really want to hear. We do not like to be told that our worship services and spiritual disciplines are primarily for our benefit and not for God's.

Acts of Worship Are Not Enough! [The Resolution]

But the prophet had another point to make. The kind of fasting God desired was not the kind the people were performing, but a "fast" that consisted in feeding the hungry, housing the homeless, and clothing the naked. The purpose of this kind of service was to relieve suffering. If the people fasted in order to share their food with the hungry, that was a service acceptable to God. Spiritual discipline for its own sake was barren, but spiritual discipline for the sake of others bore genuine fruit.

The books of the prophets are filled with criticism of people who are careful in their religious performances but careless about works of love and justice. Hear Amos's words: "I hate, I despise your festivals, and I take no delight in your solemn assemblies . . . but let justice roll down like waters, and righteousness as an everflowing stream" (Amos 5:21-24). The prophetic point is clear: acts of worship are not enough. No one serves God truly who only engages in worship, and does not also perform deeds of love and justice toward those in need.

Down through the ages, we have found it difficult to remember that God does not need our worship services, our hymns of praise, our study of scripture, or even our prayers. To be sure, worship is a fundamental resource for faith, for both the community and the individual. It is a sacrament of God's love, through which the life of the community is renewed and sustained. Worship enables the covenant community to fulfill its vocation as the sacrament of God's love for the rest of the world. But God requires more of us than worship. God requires us to help the needy and oppressed.

Why do we, the covenant people, keep getting it wrong? Why is it so easy to believe that God is pleased with our worship and spiritual discipline, and so hard to acknowledge that God cares most about the homeless, the oppressed, the hungry, and those who don't fit into mainstream society? It is peculiar that the more satisfied we become with our worship and the buildings made for worship, the less room we find in our lives for those who live on the edges of society, the people with whom we are uncomfortable, whom we don't really want in our homes, in our neighborhoods, and especially, in our congregations.

Service Acceptable to God [The New Possibility]

God does not require us to solve the vast problems of suffering, world hunger, homelessness, and poverty once and for all. That is not the point. The prophets did not know how to solve those problems in their time, and no one knows how to do so in our time. But the prophets were not daunted by the size or persistence of the problems.

The prophetic point is this: the God who creates the covenant community is unwavering in commitment to the oppressed, the needy, and the suffering. God demands that we help those in desperate need, and that we cry out on behalf of those who suffer in silence. We are God's co-workers, God's hands and feet in the world. When the church gives up on the poor and the needy, it gives up on God. When the church's worship and spiritual discipline serve us and not God, then the light of our witness grows dim. The only way the people of God can walk faithfully in God's path is to share our food with the hungry, clothe the naked, loose the bonds of oppression and injustice, and even shelter the homeless in our homes! This is a hard word for us who are comfortable. But, for the whole covenant people, the question of the oppressed, the hungry, and the homeless is a question about who God is and who we are before God. We cannot ignore this question and keep our integrity as the people of God. Answering it effectively requires imagination, resourcefulness, and a great deal of dedication. Most of us have heavy enough burdens without this. But the authenticity and vitality of the church's ministry are at stake.

The prophetic summons of Isaiah 56, and the promise that goes with it, are even deeper and broader than we have noted up to this point. Right after the passage we have quoted, in the very next verses, the prophet expresses the core of his summons and promise:

> If you pour out your *soul* for the hungry,
>   and satisfy the *soul* of the afflicted,
> Then your light shall shine in the darkness,
>   and your gloom shall be like the noonday.
> The Lord will guide you continually,
>   and satisfy your soul in parched places. . . .
> You shall be like a watered garden,
>   like a spring of water that never fails.
>   (Isa. 58:10-11 author translation)

It is not merely our food that we are called to share with the hungry and afflicted, but *ourselves*. That is what the Hebrew word for "soul" means. We are summoned to share ourselves with the afflicted, spiritually as well as materially, so that they and we together may be satisfied by the gifts that God provides us so abundantly. Ultimately, this sharing of souls, of selves, is a mutual sharing. We share ourselves and our substance with others, but we receive from them at the same time. The prophet's summons to share with the neediest is not only a responsibility but also a privilege. It is one of the chief gifts of life in the covenant community.

4. GOD AND RELIGIOUS LANGUAGE

The lingering effects of patriarchy on the life and witness of the church are a serious ethical problem, because the unequal treatment of women and men wherever it occurs, contradicts God's love for all persons. Women today are asking for equal rights, opportunities, and responsibilities, in the church as well as elsewhere. One of the most important of these rights for women is the right to share in the naming of God. However, some in the church feel personally threatened by this demand, or believe that traditional religious values will be undermined if it is met. There is fear, in particular, over changing traditional religious language, in which masculine terms for God predominate, to the virtual exclusion of feminine terms.

Is there any relevant word from the prophets on this issue? The prophets do not address the problem of sexual—or gender—discrimination, which has only recently been recognized as a problem. However, the prophets' repeated call for justice for the helpless members of society and the victims of oppression is relevant in principle to every sort of oppression. The prophets themselves did not perceive that women's lives were restricted by patriarchy; however, we are able to do so, and thus can apply the prophets' moral principles to this recently acknowledged moral problem. The relevant theological theme is the recognition of God's special love for the oppressed, which is expressed above all in the exodus story, but also in many of the other biblical texts.

There is also help to be found in the prophetic books with regard to the use of language about God. The wide range of metaphors employed in their writings provides a model for contemporary usage. The prophets show great freedom and creativity in the choice of terms for God and avoid doctrinaire fixation on any particular terms.

One of the few biblical texts, in the prophetic books or elsewhere, to speak clearly about the equal status of women and men among the people of God is Joel 2:27-29. In this well-known eschatological prophecy, the writer asserts that one day God's Spirit will be poured out upon everyone, without regard for gender, age, or social status: sons and daughters, old and young, male and female slaves, will all be empowered to give leadership and direction to God's people, for that is what the Spirit of God does, according to this prophetic witness.

For our sermon we have chosen a group of texts in the book of Hosea which show the prophet's creative and flexible use of metaphors to proclaim the gift and demand of God's love, as well as Hosea's embodiment of love in his actions toward his wife.

Our understanding of the role of metaphors in the language of religious communities is indebted to Janet Martin Soskice's probing analysis in *Metaphor and Religious Language*, as well as G. B. Caird's *The Language and Imagery of the Bible*.

The structure of the sermon. The following sermon follows the problem-resolution-new possibility paradigm. The first part states the problem and places it in its setting in the story of Hosea (*How Can We Speak About God?*). Part two describes Hosea's prophetic response—the resolution (*Vital Knowledge of God's Love*). The third part suggests the human possibilities opened up by his message (*Love Proclaimed and Embodied in Life*).

The Language of God's Love: A Sermon on Hosea

When God first spoke through Hosea, God said, "Go take for yourself a wife of whoredom and have children of whoredom, for the land commits great whoredom by forsaking the Lord." So he went and took Gomer the daughter of Diblaim, and she conceived and bore him a son. . . . The Lord said to me again, "Go, love a woman who has a lover and is an adulteress, just as the Lord loves the people of Israel, though they turn to other gods." On that day, says the Lord, . . . I will make for you a covenant . . . and I will take you for my wife in righteousness and in justice, in steadfast love and mercy. I will take you for my wife in faithfulness, and you shall know the Lord. (Hosea 1:2-3; 3:1; 2:16-20)

How Can We Speak About God? [The Problem]

How can we employ our finite language, which is shaped by our limited experience and our culture, to speak about the living God? What metaphors are adequate to proclaim the good news of God's love? This problem is as old as history, but it troubles us more deeply than ever today because we know more about the pain and injustice caused by the traditional language used to describe God. We mean, of course, the patriarchal language that permeates the Bible and the church's teaching.

The problem is urgent today, because many women feel excluded and diminished by this language, and yet others in the church fear that changing the traditional language used for God will lead to disintegration of the religious community and loss of something essential to our faith in God. Thus the debate over how we should speak about God grows ever more rancorous and bitter.

Why should we turn to Hosea for help on this question? Can a male prophet from an ancient patriarchal society help us

understand the love of God today, without reinforcing discrimination against women? Let us consider his proclamation of
God's love to see whether his witness can help us revitalize our
own witness.

Vital Knowledge of God's Love [The Resolution]

A man of his time and place, Hosea probably did not perceive
that women's lives were restricted by patriarchy. Nor did he
realize that patriarchy tainted his metaphors. Yet his witness of
faith in God can still be redemptive, for women as well as men.

Hosea's vital knowledge of God is expressed in an abundance
of metaphors. His oracles are among the most colorful and
varied among the prophets in their use of these figures of
speech. But Hosea did more than speak about God in varied
metaphors. He also embodied the message of God's chastening
and redeeming love in his own life, particularly in his relationship with his wife.

As he proclaimed the message of God and Israel, Hosea lived
his life in a manner that symbolized the reality of God's love. We
remember the story of his marriage to a prostitute named Gomer,
and we remember Gomer's infidelity to him, but we may not
remember the message of God's love that was so central to the
prophet's life and marriage. Hosea believed himself called by God
to marry and to love Gomer. And we know that although Gomer
entered into the marriage, she did not accept the limits of the
marriage covenant. She continued to take lovers. Still, Hosea
remained faithful to her and tried to evoke her faithfulness in
return. Thus Hosea's life became a symbol of God's love for Israel.
He spoke of God's relationship with the covenant community as a
marriage between husband and wife, and compared God's marriage to Israel with his own marriage to Gomer. He spoke of the
covenant community as God's family. These metaphors are so
memorable that they have become part and parcel of our thoughts
about God and the community of faith.

Nevertheless, we should not take Hosea's metaphors literally
in thinking about our relationship with God. We are dependent
upon God in a way that spouses and children are not dependent
upon one another. God alone is our creator and redeemer. And

God loves us in a way that no spouse or parent can ever love. Family relationships are thus quite different from our relationship with God. Yet, as a prophet Hosea felt called to embody his message of God's love in his own marriage, although this decision must have brought him personal suffering and derision. Yet he hoped that his love for Gomer would make God's love a reality in her life, evoking her love and faithfulness in return. In his marriage to Gomer he expressed dimensions of love that were also present in God's covenantal relation with Israel.

Hosea preached that Israel's loss of the knowledge of God was the cause of the nation's social disintegration. Knowing and trusting God's love, as gift and responsibility, are the wellsprings of righteousness. Without this knowledge and trust, human relationships collapse, and the community disintegrates. But this was not the only word Hosea proclaimed. His message, as he preached it and lived it, was that God never gives up trying to rekindle people's love in return. Hosea's commitment to Gomer exemplified God's unbreakable commitment to the covenant community.

Hosea's message ends with the assurance of God's unwavering, compassionate love. He speaks first of God's love as a husband's love for a faithless wife:

> On that day, says the Lord, I will make for you a covenant . . . and I will take you for my wife in righteousness and in justice, in steadfast love and mercy. I will take you for my wife in faithfulness, and you shall know the Lord. (2:18-20)

This does not mean that God's love is partial and inconstant, like human love. God's renewed covenant with Israel is based on God's unfailing love, and it requires Israel's love in return, love expressed in faith in God and in works of love and justice.

Hosea also speaks of God's love for Israel as the love of a *mother* for her intractable child. This picture of God as a nurturing mother is in one of the most famous passages in the prophetic books:

> When Israel was a child I loved him, and out of Egypt I called my son. . . . I took them up in my arms, but they did not know that I healed them. I led them with cords of human kindness, with

bands of love. I was to them like those who lift infants to their cheeks. I bent down, to them and fed them. . . . How can I give you up . . . O Israel? My heart recoils within me; my compassion grows warm and tender. (11:1-8)

Despite Israel's obstinate refusal to love God and be faithful in return, God's love is unceasing, always working to bring about redemption. The crucial point in this parable, as in Hosea's parable of the marriage, is not the particular choice of a metaphor, but the reality of God's love which it suggests.

We are not told whether Gomer ever understood Hosea's love and responded to it from the depths of her heart. Nor do we know whether the people of Israel to whom Hosea spoke ever understood God's love and responded to it as Hosea hoped they would. The Israelites were taken into exile, stripped of their families, their homes, and their land, and other prophets arose during the years of their exile to preach the message of God's grace. But in this prophetic tradition Hosea's words stand out. He understood the gift and claim of God's love deeply, and he proclaimed this love vividly. With an abundance of metaphors he reminded the people of Israel of the reality of the living God. He spoke of God not only as a husband and a mother, but also as a lion roaring to its cubs, as an evergreen tree giving shelter, and, in relation to God's judgment, as a rotting disease or the plague of death. Hosea clearly understood that words taken from our everyday life can speak of God's relationship to people, and he used these words as metaphors, boldly conveying the message of God's chastening and redeeming love.

Hosea's vital knowledge of God enabled him to use this abundance of metaphors to convey his message. Yet, for Hosea, words about God were not enough, and his act of love toward his unfaithful wife was a living symbol of God's love.

Love Proclaimed and Embodied in Life [The New Possibility]

Like the ancient Israelites addressed by the prophet Hosea, we also need a renewal of our knowledge of the living God in our personal and communal life. Like the ancient Israelites, we need to stop abusing one another. We must turn from the idols of personal and parochial interest and return to the one true

God. Secure in the knowledge of the gift and demand of God's love, we, too, can herald the message of God's love with our lips and in our lives.

What language shall we use to speak about God's love? Our spoken witness is not merely the passive expression of something that transcends language. It is an active force, which shapes our being and our action. Our spoken witness matters. Repeated again and again, and reinforced in the music and ritual of our corporate worship, our language about God touches us deeply and has a lasting effect upon our attitudes and feelings, as well as our ideas and behavior. As a covenant people we are responsible for our language and its effects upon people, including our language about God. We must not fix our speech rigidly in the metaphors of the past, for to do this is to perpetuate the injustices of a patriarchal society. Instead, we must free our speech to reflect the freedom of God's grace. The love of God works wonders in our life, showing us the limitations and failures of past forms of service, and guiding us to new forms of service for a new age. The metaphors of the past reflect ancient understandings, and are no longer a sufficient expression of our witness to the living God. We need not abandon them entirely, but we must not absolutize them. The possibilities of speaking truly about God's love are endless, just as the possibilities of embodying God's love in our human relationships are endless.

Our witness to God's love must be embodied in our lives just as Hosea's was. And it must also be expressed in ways that convey the full meaning of God's equal love for all God's people, women as well as men. May a vital knowledge of God's love set us free today to proclaim this love in our speech, as well as to embody it in our lives, with the same creativity that we discover in the witness of Hosea.

5. THE HIERARCHY AND THE LAITY IN THE CHURCH'S MINISTRY

Institutionalism is under attack in our culture today, and ecclesial hierarchies are a primary target, because they are perceived as the guardians of traditional structures and the opponents of needed change. The more authoritarian the church's structure, the more it is criticized. The issues of ministry and authority are complex, and the outcome of current controversies is impossible to predict. Governance and leadership are such important parts of church life and the variations on them so many, that no single recommendation could possibly solve all the problems. Furthermore, the pulpit is not an appropriate setting to deal with most of these problems. However, it is appropriate to preach on the implications of the prophetic witness for our understanding of leadership in the church. This is a difficult problem for preaching, because preachers belong to the hierarchy of the church, and may therefore appear defensive. Self-awareness is in order. This is not to suggest that clergy cannot be critical of institutional structures and policies, for of course they can be, even though they benefit from them.

The fullest comments in the prophetic writings on the role of the priestly and royal officials in the life of the covenant community are found in the books of Isaiah, Hosea, and Jeremiah. Most of these comments are critical of the priests and kings. *Isaiah* proclaimed the judgment of God against the kingdom of King Ahaz, partly because he paid no attention to Isaiah's oracles (Isa. 7–8). Later, Isaiah, or a disciple, described the ideal leader of Israel who contrasted strongly with Ahaz (Isa. 11:1-5). The anointed leader is imbued with the knowledge and fear of God, and rules justly and with discernment. This famous messianic text is the most concise prophetic statement of the understanding of the source and aim of leadership among the people of God.

Hosea condemned the priests and the kings of Israel for their godlessness and destructive leadership (Hos. 4:4-6; 5:1-2; 7:1-7; 8:4-6), and *Jeremiah* did the same for the priests and kings of Judah a century later (Jer. 21:11–22:30). Hosea's oracles have nothing positive to say about the officials of Israel, but Jeremiah alludes once to King Josiah's righteous rule (Jer. 22:15-16). One of the most interesting passages on this subject is the account of *Amos's* encounter with the chief priest of the temple of Bethel during the reign of Jeroboam I. This is a classic case of confrontation between the official hierarchy and a prophet of God (Amos 7:10-17). It is the text we have chosen to preach on, because it illustrates the perennial tension between the hierarchy and their critics so vividly. The point that we make in our sermon is that God not only speaks through those who hold regular priestly authority in the church, but also through faithful persons who do not, and that the witness of such persons is indispensable to the integrity of the church's ministry.

Every social group or organization, from the family to the nation, finds that some kind of hierarchy, or body of persons in authority, is important for its continuous existence. We think the question is not whether or not to have a hierarchy but what kind of hierarchy to have, and how it can be made responsive to the other members of the group and to new needs and conditions that develop in the course of the group's life. We do not infer from the prophets' criticism of the hierarchy of Israel that they were opposed to hierarchical authority as such, any more than we infer from their criticism of Israel's ritual behavior that they were opposed to ritual as such. Their criticism is directed at abuses of authority and corruptions of ritual.

A fundamental theological consideration in answering the question of the legitimacy of a particular structure of leadership in the church is that the covenant community is God's creation, while all particular structures of leadership in the community are human creations. More often than not these structures resemble those abroad in secular society at the time they are created. These particular structures have no permanent divine sanction but are temporary expedients, always subject to reassessment and change. Although some form of representative leadership is crucial for the church to function, no particular form can claim theological sanction.

The structure of the sermon. The problem addressed by the sermon is the conflict in the covenant community over the quality of leadership rendered by those in authority (*Conflict with the Hierarchy*). The resolution is acceptance by the laity of God's call to share in the community's prophetic ministry (*The Prophetic Vocation of the Laity*). And the new possibility is *The Shared Ministry of Clergy and Laity*.

HIERARCHY AND THE FAITHFUL WITNESS
OF THE LAITY: A SERMON ON AMOS 7

Then Amaziah, the priest of Bethel, sent to King Jeroboam of Israel, saying, "Amos has conspired against you in the very center of the house of Israel; the land is not able to bear all his words." And Amaziah said to Amos, "O seer, go, flee away to the land of Judah, earn your bread there, and prophesy there; but never again prophesy at Bethel, for it is the king's sanctuary, and it is a temple of the kingdom." Then Amos answered Amaziah, "I am no prophet, nor a prophet's son; but I am a herdsman, and a dresser of sycamore trees, and the Lord took me from following the flock, and the Lord said to me, 'Go, prophesy to my people Israel.'" (Amos 7:10-15)

Conflict with the Hierarchy [The Problem]

Criticism of hierarchical leaders is as old as time and as universal as the human community, but it is especially vigorous in the church at the present time. The hierarchy is very unpopular today. In fact, the very existence of a hierarchy is being challenged in some quarters. This dissatisfaction with the leadership of the church is matched by public dissatisfaction with government officials. It is also a troubled time for corporate executives and university presidents. Is the criticism fair, or is it merely an aggressive reaction to frustration over the size and complexity of our institutions?

Institutional leadership is ambiguous, even in the church. On the one hand, it is indispensable. No organization can do its work without it. The church's hierarchy performs functions that are crucial to its life and mission. But, on the other hand, intitutional leaders can easily become preoccupied with the maintenance and preservation of institutional structures and can resist change, especially when their positions of power and privilege are threatened. When others believe change is needed, conflict occurs. That is what is happening in the church today. Many people in the church are calling for change, so that the church can minister more effectively to society's changing needs, and to the many new voices crying out for help. Some view the church's hierarchy as an obstacle to the church's mission in the world, while others defend it as central to the church's continuity and integrity.

This conflict between the established hierarchy and the voices of change is mirrored in the Bible. It is exemplified above all in the story of Jesus' passion, and it is reflected in the stories of the prophets of Israel as well. The prophets recognized the ambiguity in the relation of the covenant community to its hierarchical leaders. Most of them were not regular members of the priesthood in authority in the sanctuaries. They were called by God to their prophetic role independently of the hierarchical structures. They were called to prophesy to the whole community of Israel, but they found themselves in confrontation with the regular hierarchy, who tried to silence them. The story of Amos stands out as the classic case.

Amos the layman was blunt in his criticism of the hierarchy of Israel. He proclaimed what he believed was important to God, although it was not what those in authority wanted to hear. In reply, the authorities directed him to leave: not merely to find another congregation in which to preach, or another denomination in which to minister, but to get out of the country! We do not know what happened to Amos, but we do know what happened to the authorities, for they fell when the kingdom fell, just as Amos warned that they would.

The Prophetic Vocation of the Laity [The Resolution]

Amos was a layman who made his living herding sheep and tending sycamore trees. He was not professionally trained for leadership in the temple, and he had no official authority there. God took him from his work on the land and sent him to the principal temple of Israel to remind the priests there of their true service of God and the real needs of God's people.

Amos was one of many persons who were called by God to lead the covenant community back to its true vocation and who were critical of those in authority in the sanctuaries of Israel. Hosea was another, and Isaiah, Micah, and Jeremiah. In the Hebrew Bible it is usually lay people, those not in official positions of authority, who speak as the conscience of Israel. The Bible acknowledges the importance of the official priesthood, and it contains a good many regulations for its maintenance. It goes to great lengths to insure that the people will support the priests with their offerings. But when it comes to calling the congregation of Israel back to its true vocation under God, it is usually lay persons who do this. It is clear the prophetic voice of the laity is indispensable to the authentic ministry of the people of God.

Lay voices are important not only in the Hebrew Bible; all the prophetic voices that are identified in the New Testament are the voices of laity, from Jesus and his disciples to Paul. It may not be fair to the later priestly hierarchy to use this as a standard, for the church in New Testament times was a loosely organized community awaiting the end of the age. Ordinary institutional structures were unnecessary in a world that was not going to last. But when the world went on and on, and the present age did not end, the church had to organize itself for the long term, and then it appointed presbyters and bishops to govern its life and lead its mission. This priestly hierarchy has lasted up to the present in a variety of forms, and it will surely endure as long as the church itself. But we must also affirm that, as long as the church endures, God will raise up prophetic voices from among the laity to recall the people of God, including those in regular positions of authority, to their true vocation.

The Shared Ministry of Clergy and Laity [The New Possibility]

The voice of the laity is a means of grace. Through the prophetic witness of the laity, God purifies, re-creates, and empowers the covenant community. The faithful witness of the clergy is indispensable, too, that goes without saying. But the witness of the clergy is not enough. The clergy itself must be continually called to account, and the experience of centuries has shown that it is the laity who do this above all. It is the faithful witness of the whole people, the *laos* of God, that determines the quality of the church's life and ministry. God has called lay people from Amos's time to our own to be a means of grace, to recall the church to its true vocation.

Amos and Isaiah, Micah and Jeremiah were deeply commited members of the covenant community. Their faith was shaped by the community's traditions, and their religious language was learned in the sanctuaries of Israel. They shared in Israel's worship, and they cared about Israel's survival in a hostile world. They cared as much as the priestly hierarchy. They cared enough to evaluate the leadership candidly against covenantal standards of justice and righteousness, and by doing this they helped renew Israel's fidelity to God again and again. That is part of the ministry to which clergy and laity alike are called by God today. The laity have an indispensable role to play in the church's great drama of obedience to God. And bearing prophetic witness is an essential aspect of the laity's role. We should all rejoice in God's calling of the laity to this responsibility and thank God for their faithful witness.

6. THE NEW COVENANT AND JUDAISM

The problem this sermon addresses is Christian anti-Semitism, which has existed from the beginning of the church until today. It has had devasting effects upon the Jewish people, particularly in this century, and it has corrupted the souls of Christians. It has also deepened the separation between Christians and Jews and their cultures, to our mutual impoverishment.

Many Christians and Jews are acutely aware of the problem today, and are offering possible solutions. One thing they are doing is writing books. The following books, which we recommend, are among them: *Christians and Jews: A Troubled Family*, by Walter Harrelson and Randall Falk; *To Mend the World*, by Emil L. Fackenheim; and *Faith and Fratricide* by Rosemary Radford Ruether. Falk and Fackenheim are Jewish, Harrelson and Ruether are Christian.

A major factor contributing to Christian anti-Semitism is the supersessionist interpretation of the prophetic writings. According to this interpretation the church superseded, or replaced, the Jewish community as God's covenant people. This view is rationalized on the basis of the prophets' indictment of Israel for sinfulness and idolatry. Israel failed, so the argument goes; therefore, God created a new community in its place, and that community is the church.

There are very serious problems with the view that Christianity has replaced Judaism as the true people of God. Not only has it contributed to the horrible suffering inflicted on the Jewish people, but it is surely invalidated by history. The church has *not* displaced the Jewish people. The Jewish witness of faith has survived through the centuries and around the world. The apostle Paul's view of the relationship between the church and the synagogue is much more appropriate theologically than the supersessionist view. In Romans 11, Paul insists that God will never reject Israel as God's covenant people. He uses the metaphor of an olive tree to speak of the relationship between ancient Israel and the newborn church. Through God's gracious outpouring of the Holy Spirit, God has "grafted" new branches onto the olive tree. But the living root of the tree, which supports the branches, is Israel. Paul's metaphor makes as much sense as ever today, if Christians will only take it to heart.

There are of course no prophetic texts dealing with the subject of Christian anti-Semitism. On the other hand, there are prophetic texts that have been interpreted by Christians in such a way as to deny the continuing vocation of the Jewish people as the people of God, thus contributing to the problem of anti-Semitism. The text most often interpreted in this way is Jeremiah 31:31-34. For this reason we have chosen it as the text for our sermon.

In the text, Jeremiah promises the exiled Jewish community that God will make a new covenant with the house of Israel and the house of Judah. The typical Christian interpretation views the creation of the church as the fulfillment of this promise and identifies the broken covenant as the one between God and the Jewish people. That covenant, according to this interpretation, was based upon the performance of external works, while the Christian covenant is a spiritual one.

This interpretation of Jeremiah's intention is self-serving. Jews can and do apply Jeremiah's promise of a new covenant to themselves with equal legitimacy. Christians should not read this text as a congratulatory word about what has happened to them, on the supposition that God has succeeded with them where God failed with the Jewish people. This interpretation misconstrues the history of Judaism as well as the history of Christianity. Christians have been just as prone as Jews to externalize covenantal obedience: legalism has plagued the church in every age! And Jews have been just as likely as Christians to love God and their neighbor with all their hearts. In this respect there is no essential difference between Jewish and Christian piety, though there are many differences between Judaism and Christianity in other respects.

The structure of the sermon. This final sermon has the familiar three-part structure. The first part states the problem (*The Covenant Broken*), the second, the resolution (*Knowledge of God and the Forgiveness of Sin*), and the third, the new possibility (*The Covenant Renewed*).

God's Covenant with Jews and Christians: A Sermon on Jeremiah 31

The days are surely coming, says the Lord, when I will make a new covenant with the house of Israel and the house of Judah. It will not be like the covenant that I made with their ancestors . . . a covenant that they broke, though I was their master. . . . But this is the covenant that I will make with the house of Israel after those days. I will put my law within them, and I will write it on their hearts; and I will be their God, and they shall be my people. No longer shall they teach one another, or say to each other, "Know the Lord," for they shall all know me, from the least of them to the greatest, says the Lord, for I will forgive their iniquity, and remember their sin no more. (Jeremiah 31:31-34)

The Covenant Broken [The Problem]

The prophet Jeremiah composed this prophecy of the new covenant for the survivors of the fall of the kingdom of Judah in the sixth-century B.C.E.—for the remnant living among the ruins of Jerusalem and the exiles scattered in other lands. In the people's minds, as in Jeremiah's, the covenant between God and Israel had been broken. Their nation was destroyed, the Davidic kingship was no more, and the land given to their ancestors was no longer theirs. Many of the people blamed God for this calamity, gave up on the God of the covenant, and turned to other gods. But Jeremiah had another interpretation. He believed the fault was not God's but the people's. It was they who had broken the covenant, not God. It was their infidelity, idolatry, and injustice that had caused the destruction of the nation, and not any failure of God's. The covenant was broken, to be sure, but they were the ones who had broken it.

We tend to interpret Jeremiah's word about the broken covenant merely as a word about the past, a word about ancient Israel. This is easy to do, and it is comforting to keep it that way. We prefer to take every prophetic word of judgment as a word about other people. Surely it was not we who broke the covenant! Surely it was not we who turned away from God and broke God's law. On the contrary, we are the ones on whose hearts the law is written, the ones who truly know God and obey God's law. That is the way Christians have read this text over the years. The Jews of ancient Israel were the ones who broke the covenant, not we!

Jeremiah's word was first addressed to particular Jews at a particular time in history. But his word was also relevant for later generations of Jews and Christians. And it is a living word for us as well. The broken covenant is not only the covenant broken by others. It is ours as well. The broken covenant is the reality of unfaithfulness and injustice in our own lives! In our own hearts we have lost a vital knowledge of God. Our own faith is dim. We are people who settle comfortably into religious legalism. We have to be taught by others; we have a second-hand faith, which depends on what other people tell us about the gifts of God's Spirit and about God's will for our lives. We may think that the covenant is written on our hearts, but is it?

Knowledge of God and the Forgiveness of Sin *[The Resolution]*

What is the way to a vital knowledge of God, a knowledge written on the heart? According to Jeremiah it is grace and forgiveness. There can be no vital knowledge of God unless God bestows God's Spirit upon us. And there can be no vital knowledge of God unless we turn to God and receive forgiveness. We must search our conscience and repent of all that blocks the Spirit of God in our hearts and lives.

God's forgiveness is always available, and the promise of forgiveness encourages us to seek God's mercy and confess our sin, which is the first step in repentance and reformation of life. Hosea promised God's forgiveness to wayward Israelites in the eighth-century B.C.E., just as Jeremiah promised it to Judeans a century later. And Ezekiel and Second Isaiah after them made the same promise of God's mercy and redeeming grace. The psalms are filled with this promise, and so of course is the Christian witness of faith. We can amend our ways, deeply and truly, because we are sure of God's forgiveness and of God's empowerment in the new path of righteousness. Repentance is possible because grace is sure.

What does repentance look like concretely in our lives? Surely there are as many practical ways of repenting as there are ways of sinning! But our concern here is with Christian anti-Semitism, or Christian hatred of Jews, a hatred that seems to lie at the very heart of the Christian witness of faith. For one thing, repentance from anti-Semitism means refusing to tolerate slurs against Jewish people. It means turning our backs on ancient prejudices, lies, and stereotypes. It means regarding Jewish people as our brothers and sisters in God's covenant. It means affirming the validity of Jewish life and Jewish piety and the Jewish witness of faith in God.

The Covenant Renewed [The New Possibility]

Jeremiah did not interpret the destruction of Jerusalem and the exile as the end of God's dealings with the covenant people. Instead, he promised that God would act in the coming days to renew their covenant relationship. God would give them the heart to obey. Thus Jeremiah prophesied to the ancient Israelites that the broken covenant would be renewed by God's grace.

The renewed covenant was a promise for the people of Jeremiah's time, and this promise has been fulfilled again and again in the history of the Jewish community. It was fulfilled in the renewal of the Jewish community after the Babylonian exile, and in the expansion of Judaism into an enduring, worldwide community. Encouraged by prophets like Jeremiah and Second Isaiah, the Jews refused to surrender their faith, and they formed congregations in Judea and Galilee, in Syria and Egypt, and in Babylonia and Greece. This happened because God's law was written on their hearts. Those vital Jewish congregations continued in Asia, Africa, and Europe down to the present time, except where the Jewish people were killed or driven out. Much too often that was done by Christians.

But Jeremiah's promise of a renewed covenant is not simply a promise for the Jewish community. This promise was surely fulfilled in the hearts and minds of the first Christians who encountered the gift and claim of God's grace through Jesus Christ. And the fulfillment of the promise did not stop there, but continued in the many renewals of the church that have occurred by the working of God's Spirit up to our own time.

Perhaps Jeremiah's prophesy is not merely for Jews and Christians but for Muslims as well, who also count themselves children of Abraham and people of the covenant. Jeremiah's prophesy of the new covenant is for all the heirs of Abraham and Sarah, Moses and Miriam, Isaiah and Jeremiah, Peter and Paul, and Mary and Martha. It is for all who have broken the covenant with God and their neighbors, and for all who live in mutual hatred and distrust. "They shall all know me, from the least of them to the greatest, says the Lord; for I will forgive their iniquity, and I will remember their sin no more."

Jeremiah's prophecy is certainly a promise for us today. When we turn to God's grace, a new possibility opens for us. God's law becomes a living reality in our hearts. We no longer depend upon external instruction, for the voice of God's Spirit within us is our teacher. We know God and we serve God willingly, from the heart.

The perfect consummation of Jeremiah's new covenant, in which everyone knows God so intimately in their hearts that no one needs further instruction, is an eschatological hope, a hope for that future when, according to the prophet Isaiah, the lion will lie down with the lamb, and swords will be turned into plowshares. But this does not mean that the conditions of the new covenant are unrealizable in human experience. God's forgiveness can be appropriated truly, and human hearts can be transformed by faith. The possibility for the covenant community is the same in every age. God promises to forgive our sin and write the commandments anew on our hearts. The eternal possibility for the covenant people, for Jews and Christians alike, is that they will be given new knowledge of God's presence in their lives and that, forgiven and renewed, they will bear faithful witness to the reality of God in the world.

NOTES

Chapter 1

1. Among the relatively few works dealing with the task of preaching from the prophets, the following may be mentioned: Donald E. Gowan, *Reclaiming the Old Testament for the Christian Pulpit* (Atlanta: John Knox, 1980), pp. 119-44; Sidney Greidanus, *The Modern Preacher and the Ancient Text* (Grand Rapids: Eerdmans, 1988), pp. 228-262; James W. Cox, ed., *Biblical Preaching* (Philadelphia: Westminster, 1983), pp. 119-50; and Christopher R. Seitz, ed., *Reading and Preaching the Book of Isaiah* (Philadelphia: Fortress, 1988). James L. Crenshaw's eloquent and insightful book of sermons, *Trembling at the Threshold of a Biblical Text* (Grand Rapids: Eerdmans, 1994), contains seven sermons on prophetic texts. Two older works are now dated, but not without value: Kyle M. Yates, *Preaching from the Prophets* (Nashville: Broadman, 1942), and Andrew Blackwood, *Preaching from Prophetic Books* (New York: Abingdon-Cokesbury, 1951). On the subject of the theological and historical-critical foundations of contemporary biblical preaching, see Leander E. Keck's *The Bible in the Pulpit: The Renewal of Biblical Preaching* (Nashville: Abingdon, 1978). Two series of commentaries, *Knox Preaching Guides* and *Interpretation* (John Knox Press), are intended as aids for preaching and include volumes on the books of the prophets.

Chapter 2

1. For a fuller discussion of the nature of biblical language, see G. B. Caird, *The Language and Imagery of the Bible* (Philadelphia: Westminster Press, 1980). His treatment of metaphor comprises Part

Two (pp. 131-97). See also, Janet Martin Soskice, *Metaphor and Religious Language* (Oxford: Clarendon Press, 1985).

2. For example, Elie Wiesel, *A Jew Today* (New York: Vintage Books, 1979), pp. 3-16, and Emil L. Fackenheim, *To Mend the World: Foundations of Post-Holocaust Thought* (New York: Schocken Books, 1982), pp. 278-94.

3. For example, J. G. M. Willebrands, *Church and Jewish People: New Considerations* (New York: Paulist Press, 1992), and John M. Oesterreicher, *The New Encounter: Between Christians and Jews* (New York: Philosophical Library, 1986). The reshaping of Roman Catholic teaching concerning the relationship between the church and the Jewish people began with the Second Vatican Council. See the discussion of the relevant documents in Augustin Bea's *The Church and the Jewish People* (New York: Harper & Row, 1966).

4. See the discussion of the similarities and differences between Jews and Christians in Walter Harrelson and Randall M. Falk's book, *Jews and Christians: A Troubled Family* (Nashville: Abingdon, 1990).

5. This point is made persuasively by Donald E. Gowan in *Reclaiming the Old Testament for the Christian Pulpit* (Atlanta: John Knox, 1980), pp. 137-38. See also John C. Holbert, *Preaching Old Testament* (Nashville: Abingdon, 1991), pp. 10-12.

Chapter 3

1. Eugene L. Lowry offers a helpful critique of aspects of the lectionary as a guide for preaching in *Living with the Lectionary: Preaching through the Revised Common Lectionary* (Nashville: Abingdon, 1992). The faults he finds are mostly in the determination of individual pericopes, especially where the lection leaves a gap in the sense-unit. He does not evaluate the overall selection of texts.

2. Sidney Greidanus describes a similar process helpfully in *The Modern Preacher and the Ancient Text*, pp. 250-62, though he extends it appropriately to include the whole Bible.

3. The issues discussed here are treated in various ways in Donald E. Gowan, *Reclaiming the Old Testament for the Christian Pulpit* (Atlanta: John Knox, 1980), pp. 11-14, 121-26; Don M. Wardlaw, ed., *Preaching Biblically: Creating Sermons in the Shape of Scripture* (Philadelphia: Westminster, 1983); and Sidney Greidanus, *op. cit.*, pp. 141-56, 238-50.

4. Among the many recent treatments of the subject of narrative preaching, see John Holbert, *Preaching Old Testament* (Nashville: Abingdon, 1990), and Eugene L. Lowry, *The Homiletical Plot: The Sermon as Narrative Art Form* (Nashville: Abingdon, 1980).